The Chosen Few

DISCARD

The Chosen Few

Surviving the
Nuclear Holocaust

EDWARD MYERS

and books

South Bend, Indiana

THE CHOSEN FEW
Surviving the Nuclear Holocaust

Copyright © 1982 by Edward Myers

and books
702 South Michigan, South Bend, Indiana 46618

Library of Congress Catalog Number: 82-072604

International Standard Book Number: 0-89708-107-2

First Printing.

Printed in the United States of America

Additional copies available:
    the distributors
    702 South Michigan
    South Bend, IN 46618

To P.K.L.

Table of Contents

Acknowledgements

Many people have helped me write this book. Some of them are survivalists: Bruce Clayton, Bob Velten, Robert Himber, and Duncan Long, especially, but also CA1, CO6, MO1, NM1, and Marc. Others who assisted in the project are non-survivalists and sometimes even anti-survivalists: Robert Jay Lifton, Henry Coppolillo, Evan Peelle, John E. Mack, Chris Zafiratos, Robert Ristinen, John Birks, and J. Frank Mollner. Yet as much as these people have done to help, the ones who made the biggest difference were my friends Paige and Walt, Denis and Susan, Mike and Ann, Eddie and Janet, Paul Z., Jim B., Kay, Anita, Mindy, Tamara, Anne, Barry, and of course Edith, who suggested my doing the book in the first place.

In every age man faces a pervasive theme which defies his engagement and yet must be engaged. In Freud's day it was sexuality and moralism. Now it is unlimited technological violence and absurd death. We do well to name the threat and to analyze its components. But our need is to go further, to create new psychic and social forms to enable us to reclaim not only our technology, but our very imaginations, in the service of the continuity of life.

—Robert Jay Lifton
Death in Life: Survivors of Hiroshima

Introduction

Remember the Grasshopper and the Ant? The Grasshopper fiddled and danced all day while the Ant toiled in preparation for winter. When winter came, the Ant enjoyed the fruits of his toil and the Grasshopper ended up hungry and cold. "Won't you help me?" asked the Grasshopper. But the Ant told him, "No — you must dance in winter to the tune you played all summer."

Lately, millions of Americans have been acting out this Ant-and-Grasshopper routine, although so far without the clear outcome in Aesop's fable. The "ants" call themselves survivalists and go about preparing for currency collapse and World War III. The "grasshoppers" (at least according to the ants) are everybody else. The ants store food, buy gold coins, build fallout shelters, and sometimes learn to use HK91 heavy assault rifles. The grasshoppers take vacations to Paris and Disneyworld. The ants think the grasshoppers are fools. The grasshoppers think the ants are crackpots. Nobody knows what's going to happen, but everyone knows that the other guy's *got* to be wrong.

One thing for sure: the Ant-and-Grasshopper routine will be around for a while. Survivalism is increasingly popular in this country.

Who are the survivalists, and what are they trying to survive?
The answers vary more than most people realize.

— J.W. and K.W., husband and wife, both in their late fifties,
worry about the American economy. They figure that another
depression is almost inevitable. In response to this prospect, they
have acquired a year's supply of dehydrated food to carry them
through hard times.

— H.C. fears that the United States "could be subject to a sudden nuclear attack from the Soviets." He has therefore built a fallout shelter, stocked it, and taught survival skills to his wife and
children, who "take part enthusiastically."

— M.R. is a newspaper reporter in central Iowa. "I am a born-
again Christian," he says, "and I think our age is just about over."
Getting ready for what he and others call the Tribulation, he is accumulating guns. He currently owns three handguns, three shotguns,
and a couple of military assault rifles.

— The Bishop of a Mormon church in Colorado, G.H. stores
food for his family. But he explains, "If someone were to come to my
door demanding food, I'd give it to him. Our church doesn't believe
in guns."

Not all survivalists are self-taught commandos lurking behind
crates of freeze-dried chicken tetrazzini. Those I have interviewed include young couples, Mormon families, university professors, senior
citizens, mountain hermits, yogis, and businessmen. Many are entirely harmless. Few want to deal with any crisis more demanding
than what their day-to-day lives present. There is, however, a militant
minority, and it appears to be growing. This minority warrants
genuine concern. Yet as usual, the fanatics are among the most
vocal and "newsworthy," thereby distorting the overall picture.
Nobody wants to watch a TV documentary about retired folks
who store beans, rice, and powdered milk under the bed. The gun
fanatics in the camouflage garb draw much more attention. The
fact remains, however, that most survivalists — at least for the time
being — don't fit the popular stereotype.

What all survivalists share is a belief that something terrible will
happen soon, and that people had better get ready for it. Specific concerns vary according to the individual survivalists; plans for how to
get ready vary still more. The most consistent worries are inflation, oil
embargoes, economic collapse, racial conflict, ecological disaster, and

especially nuclear war — in short, much of what worries nearly everyone during the final decades of the Twentieth Century. Where the survivalists differ from non-survivalists is in their response to these concerns. Most survivalists believe that the problems facing us defy solution, yet they resent their helplessness and want to overcome it; since they can't save the world, they figure on saving themselves.

Perhaps this is nothing new. Some people have always worried about their vulnerability and have done whatever they could to compensate for it. Although Aesop's fable of the Ant and the Grasshopper may not be as appropriate to the survival movement as some ot its members imagine, neither is it irrelevant; and it suggests something about how long a debate has raged between persons who brace themselves for the coming of hard times and those who don't. More recent eras also indicate certain precedents. The exploration and settlement of the United States was at least partly the expression of a survivalist mentality. Relatively self-sufficient individuals and small groups established themselves in an unfamiliar and often dangerous land, sometimes at the risk of their own or the communal wellbeing, and tried to endure. Whether this heritage — especially in it more violent aspects — is to the modern survivalists' advantage seems questionable at best; but the tradition is hard to ignore. In recent decades, the predecessors of today's survivalists have worried many people. The bomb shelter fad of the late 1950s and early '60s, for instance, with its unanswered question about neighbors' willingness to shoot each other, suggested that Americans might end up as dangerous to each other as their supposed enemies.

Meanwhile, whatever the origins or consequences of the survival movement, it continues to grow. Some of the growth is a result of general uncertainties. The American economy remains unstable; our way of life continues to depend on the flow of mideastern oil; even short-term stability produces long-term problems like pollution and the depletion of resources. All these interlocking risks can make even the sunniest Pollyanna wonder how long our civilization will last. Yet unquestionably what stimulates the survival movement the most is the risk of nuclear war. The outlook for such a war "is quite surprisingly grim," as British scientist Nigel Calder stated recently. "The risk of a holocaust is growing with every year that passes, and whether we shall avoid it between now and 1990 is at least questionable." This will hardly come as news to anyone. The fear of nuclear war is in everyone's thoughts these days, whether openly discussed or not.

Public controversies over Ground Zero Week, civil defense programs, and Jonathan Schell's book *The Fate of the Earth* are only one form which the fear takes. Another form is survivalism.

Nobody knows exactly how widespread the survival movement is. The reason is simple. Most survivalists regard their safety as paramount, and they also regard anonymity and safety as interdependent. Many prefer not to let anyone — sometimes even their own relatives — know of their activities. It's possible that no one will ever know in detail who the survivalists are, where they live, and what they are doing. On the other hand, certain kinds of evidence can mark off at least the contours of growth. Sales of survival supplies provide one indicator. Proliferation of survivalist magazines, books, and newsletters is another. Word of mouth is a third. These are crude and approximate; but in assessing a secretive subculture, such measures may give the best indicators possible.

What will come of the survival movement? This, too, nobody knows for sure. Perhaps the survivalists will become a major trend in American culture. Perhaps they will fade like their predecessors during the 1960s. Perhaps — who knows? — they'll be the only people around in a few years.

My intention in writing this book is to provide an overview of the survival movement, but with special emphasis on those persons and groups concerned with nuclear war. Many people regard the survivalists as a lunatic fringe; I am convinced that they amount to considerably more than that. They merit close attention. Although survivalists may account for a small minority of Americans, their number is growing. More important, even this minority has a potential for influencing others — perhaps everyone. Skeptics may well question this potential. Survivalists are way out in the boondocks, right? How can they affect *anyone*? One reason is simply that not all survivalists are off hiding in the woods. Another reason is that survivalists may become a potentially significant lobby within the American political arena. There are indications already, for instance, that survivalists wish to influence government policy on civil defense. The last (and perhaps most important) reason is that survivalists already swing considerable symbolic weight; they have drawn public attention much as people do when lowering their lifeboat from the deck of an ocean liner. It's possible that survivalists will influence how we Americans see ourselves, our problems, and our ability to solve them. Trying to understand the survival movement may help us to understand our present and future.

This is not, however, a sociological study. I almost wish it were: the survival movement would be a sociologist's dream and nightmare. (Dream because the movement is fascinating; nightmare because formal research by an outsider would be almost impossible.) The fact remains that my approach here is strictly anecdotal. If someone else can persuade survivalists to pour out their statistical soul, I'll be more than happy to see the results. I question the likelihood of anyone succeeding at this, however; most survivalists are reluctant to speak with outsiders under any circumstances. (There's a partial study by a survivalist writer along sociological lines, however — more on this later.)

One way or another, I have tried to portray the survivalists, to let them flesh out the portrait themselves, and then to make some kind of sense of who they are and what they mean. I am convinced that the outcome will suggest something about our chances of survival not just as individuals, but also as a culture.

Chapter One

Who Are the Survivalists?

Snapshot: man with a gun. Smiling at the camera, he holds a military assault rifle slightly elevated and pointed to the left. He's wearing a camouflage-pattern shirt, sleeves rolled up, front unbuttoned, tails out. He looks ready for anything. But the scene around him is, if anything, idyllic: well-kept lawns, oaks and maples, clear autumn sky beyond the New England village in the background.

Who is this man? Like most of his kindred spirits, he wants to remain anonymous. But almost any American who watches TV or reads the newspapers could identify him at once. He's a survivalist. The gun, the "cammy" outfit... This man isn't about to let even Doomsday slow him down. If the bombs start to fall, he's got his shelter. If he makes it through the attack, he's got his emergency food and supplies. But if *you* should somehow survive, too, don't come running. The survivalist has guns and ammo set aside just for irresponsible Grasshoppers like you.

And within the past few years, the survivalist has entered the popular imagination alongside other quintessential Americans — the pioneer, the cowboy, the vigilante — who supposedly exemplify the great national virtues of independence and cleverness and durability. This image has made the survivalist an object both of admiration and fear. Some people see the survivalist as Life, Liberty, and the Pursuit of Happiness incarnate. Others see him as a mere sociopath.

Stereotypes sometimes contain an element of truth; or at least certain individuals within the group end up fitting the stereotype. This is true for the survivalists. Some of them *do* imagine themselves to be the new frontiersmen — pioneers who will explore and tame the post-holocaust world. Among these, some expect years of lawlessness, and they prepare accordingly just to be safe. A minority appears almost eager to see the day when laws, social restrictions, and even basic taboos collapse. But for the most part, the survivalists are individually less dramatic and extreme than the generalizations about them suggest. Many dread nuclear war and other possible disasters as much as non-survivalists; whatever they anticipate for the future, most live rather ordinary — even banal — lives in the here and now. The stereotype of the survivalist as a paramilitary nut is a risky oversimplification.

The purpose of this chapter is to provide a more detailed sense of who the survivalists are, what they believe, and what they do. This is, of course, the purpose of the whole book as well. But before proceeding to examine specific issues and the survivalists' responses to them, we should consider the range of personalities and backgrounds which give the movement its flesh and blood. In some respects, there is no single "survival movement," however convenient it may be to speak of one. There are many activities, concerns, beliefs, fears, and assumptions which take shape in different ways within different people's behavior. The variety and range of survivalists makes it all the more important to focus attention not just on patterns, but also on individuals who make up the patterns.

In order to provide this focus, I've spent much of the past year contacting and interviewing survivalists. Many have hesitated to speak with me — even over the phone — fearing violation of their privacy. Others have refused any contact whatever. One elderly couple wrote to me, objecting to my supposed detachment from life-and-death issues: "we have another 230,000,000 of these types in the USA that theorize, fantasize, temporize, Ostrichsize (sic), and any other type of response except *doing something about the problem to take care of themselves.*" And that was that. Still others, however, responded to my request for information (though cautiously at first) and wrote, telephoned, or arranged to speak with me in person about their beliefs and activities. The result has been an extensive network of contacts. Some of the people willing to provide opinions or data have done so minimally. Perhaps three dozen have been more detailed in their descriptions. From these various contacts, I've not only acquired facts suitable for elaborating on the specific subjects in this book; I've also gotten a sense of some relatively intangible aspects of survivalism.

The following sketches serve to let several survivalists talk about themselves, their beliefs, and their activities. Subsequent chapters will examine particular issues more closely. These individuals, however, can provide a kind of overview first. Of course, these people can't speak for the full range of their fellows; and they don't even represent all survivalists whose attitudes they most nearly share. But they are nonetheless fairly typical of what appear to be sub-groups within the movement. They are also articulate. For the most part, I've therefore refrained from commenting on the speakers' own words.

R.V., 41, is a professional "survival consultant" in downstate New York. Like many survivalists, R.V. isn't concerned solely with the risk of nuclear war; and his activities haven't been a sudden, short-term phenomenon. He explains that "As a child, I was raised on a small hotel/farm. We took in guests year-round. The milk they drank and the cheese and butter they ate came from our small (thirteen) herd of cows. Whenever the cows gave birth to a bull, it was kept for nine months and then butchered. Chickens and eggs also came from our farm, as did the pork and many vegetables. Also, growing up in the country gave me a love of the land and a feeling of oneness with nature. I learned not to try to change nature but to live in harmony with her. Although we were never rich, there was always food to eat, whether home-grown or wild."

R.V. soon discovered that the world wasn't always so idyllic. "As a young adult, I went to Viet Nam — before protesting that war became fashionable. What I found there was a land which was rich agriculturally, but where malnutrition was the order of the day. I saw the young and the old trying to function on empty stomachs, and I saw first-hand the ravages of war. I quickly added military or tactical survival to my knowledge and learned how to defend, by whatever means necessary, what was rightfully mine. I also learned to live off the land and to practice those physical and emotional disciplines which were necessary for survival.

"Although I had all the earmarkings of a survivalist at this point," he continues, "the concept of being one hadn't entered my mind. Then, about five years ago, we bought our house. Two years prior to that, I bought a few rifles and became proficient in their use. I also redeveloped my hunting/tracking skills. When my wife and I purchased the house, I began to plant things. I put in a dozen dwarf fruit trees known for their hardiness and the storage abilities of their fruits. I also planted perennial plants such as asparagus, rhubarb, and currant bushes. Then I began to re-discover my Christian roots and again took an interest in the Bible. At this point, I began to purchase books on farming, raising animals, first aid, defense, survival and camping skills, etc. And I slowly built a catalogue file of all those companies who sold survival products of all kinds. About this time, I sold my stamp collection and used the money to buy tents, sleeping bags, extra ammunition, fishing and trapping gear, cold weather clothing, storage containers, camp and home kerosene stoves, gold coins, and finally survival foods. I also put up a supply of wines that would keep at least ten years."

So what was the upshot of all this preparation? R.V. himself was surprised. "One day, I was in the basement moving some of the items around when the enormity of what I had done struck me. Until that time, I had no idea what I was doing or why. True, I was alarmed with what was going on in the world, but I had no plan. I had become a survivalist almost as though someone else was working through me. Actually, there are a variety of survival situations. I love to hunt, fish, camp, and just plain walk in the woods, but I never forget that the instant I leave the modern world with all her conveniences and enter the wilderness, I am in a situation that could tax my survival instincts. The elderly are faced with a survival situation on a daily basis. The forces of nature can also tax us physically and emotionally. Being cut off from the nearest neighbor in a snowstorm requires special preparations. So does being stranded in a car or living next to a nuclear energy plant such as Three Mile Island. The situations requiring a survival outlook are endless and varied. I guess that being a survivalist means being in an aware and prepared frame of mind twenty-four hours a day and being able to cope with your surroundings at all times."

More recently, R.V. has felt a growing concern about the possibility of nuclear war. He states that this "is not my most immediate concern," but he also feels that "it is the possibility which troubles me the most. The reason for this is that such an event will come upon us in a flash, and the havoc and destruction will be instantaneous and widespread. I would estimate as many as sixty million killed outright, and unless people are prepared, they won't stand much of a chance for survival. The sad thing is that most people will not be prepared."

R.V. has therefore taken precautions against the risk of nuclear war. Noting that "there are certain preparations which are common to all survival situations," among them "food, water, shelter, and energy," R.V. feels that he is "ready for any emergency — including nuclear war. We live in an area which is far enough removed from any primary targets (missile silos, SAC bases, large metropolitan/industrial centers) as to afford fairly good protection from thermal blast. Our only problem would be that of fallout. Although I do not have a fallout shelter per se, it would not take long to make our basement perfectly safe. And so I must answer 'yes' to your question as to whether I could survive a nuclear war. As far as my clients go, I advise them that if they live in a primary target area, they should either get out or buy some land in a 'safe' area and develop it for emergency use. Of course it would be of use only if they could reach it before the war starts."

These survivalist beliefs and activities have changed R.V.'s life. Perhaps the degree of change wouldn't surprise too many observers; after all, the public generally acknowledges that survivalists are (no matter what else) unusually strong-minded. But an aspect of R.V.'s agenda — and that of other survivalists, too — is a kind of wider mission. R.V. explains that "since that moment (of his insight into the importance of his activities) three years ago, I have devoted my time trying to help others see what is happening around us today. Since my family is secure enough to face any situation, I feel surprisingly at ease with myself and am taking my message to any interested people. I have a strange feeling that something of immense impact is going to occur in our lifetimes and, although I really don't know what it is, I want to be prepared for any contingency." He adds, "I don't consider myself a radical or doomsday prophet, but I do feel I am being guided toward some goal, and I have decided to flow with the current."

Other survivalists take this sense of mission a step further. W.R., for example, a forty-nine-year-old computer engineer in California, has worked not only to inform people in general of his concerns, but has also convinced dozens of neighboring families to take part in various survival-oriented activities. These activities include food storage, construction of fallout shelters, and planning of defense strategies. W.R. also works as an author, lecturer, and consultant on subjects pertaining to survival.

"I've been in touch with survivalists and involved with the survival movement for some years now," he told me recently. "Some of this comes out of my Mormon background. I've been doing this for a long time. When I moved up into this community of non-Mormons, though, I realized that nobody here was prepared in any way. People didn't even have two weeks' worth of food. This got me thinking. There are a hundred and twenty-six families up here. I realized that if any sort of disaster occurred, I'd either have to share my food with them, in which case it obviously wouldn't last very long, and I and my family would probably end up starving with everybody else; or else I'd have to defend the food, which didn't appeal to me. Somebody suggested storing more food — something to hand out if need be. But that doesn't solve the problem; you give away the extra few years' food and then you're back to threatening to shoot people."

W.R.'s response was to create a third alternative. "I started speaking with my neighbors, explaining the problem. I started a newsletter. It wasn't supposed to be such a big production at first, but one thing led to another. I've had inquiries from Alaska to South Africa. This has involved a huge effort. I noticed the lack of survival equipment, so now I'm importing equipment from Hong Kong, Singapore, and other places. I also hold meetings in my home. I don't believe a single family can say, "We're survivalists, and we're going to get through.' It takes more than that. It's a community effort."

But what is the response of his neighbors to his efforts to persuade them? W.R. reports a mixed and sometimes intense reaction. "Half of the people here are angry at me. When I speak with them, some say, 'We don't like what you're doing.' So I ask them, 'What am I doing?' And they say, 'You're being divisive. You're creating a bad sense in the community.' Others say, 'I don't wish to think about disaster,' and they walk away. Others say, 'I'm prepared, but I don't want public visibility.' And of course some of the others are willing to go along."

W.R.'s activities have emphasized food storage. He has convinced half the neighboring families to store a year's supply of emergency food; he has even convinced them into storing another year's worth for the uncooperative neighbors. In addition, he has organized a smaller group of neighbors into making preparations for

defending the community in the event of a disaster. These preparations exploit the area's remoteness from major cities, but also include
training in the use of weapons. "We have selected this geographical
area carefully — a lot of people don't know about us — but we'll be
prepared if necessary. If an attack (from intruders) occurs, we plan to
intercept them two to three miles from the community. Roads can be
blocked by cutting trees with a chain saw. Then we can meet them
from carefully planned fallbacks." How cooperative are his neighbors
in this regard? W.R. explains that "Only about twelve people have
progressed to the point of considering the outcome, but this would be
sufficient."

When I asked W.R. about what events he expects to justify such
elaborate preparations, he told me, "I'm an optimist. I'm not counting
on anything happening. But my Mormon background tells me to put
that particular house in order. In terms of likelihood, I'd say that
serious economic problems — notice I don't say *collapses* — are likely
within the next few years. Also, there's a strong possibility of World
War III. It seems very likely that we'll throw some bombs at people
after they throw some at us. I'm prepared for a nuclear emergency
with our geographical placement. There are no big risks here except
for a miss. We have a blast shelter, but a good miss could take care of
us."

Still other survivalists take part in their local communities, but
not necessarily as advocates of emergency preparation. They engage
in ordinary human interchange — work, recreation, and social activities — but they intend to withdraw in a time of crisis. They are not
sociopaths. Many are, in fact, gregarious and even generous people.
But their sense of alarm at what they perceive to be the growing
dangers ahead prompts them to disengage from many commitments
and to concentrate instead on saving their own skins. At times, these
survivalists feel ambivalent about the decisions and actions which
result.

"I am a professional odds-maker of sorts," a physician in New
Mexico explained. "The medical profession is really a matter of odds-

making, in that we often balance the risk of treatment against the risk and discomfort of disease. I usually approach most life situations by trying to determine the odds. Therefore, I don't carry collision insurance on my car- the odds are in the favor of the insurance company- but I do spend some time and money preparing for various possible disasters (but only the time and money appropriate to the risk)."

This physician sees survivalism essentially as a kind of gamble — with life and death as the stakes. "I am concerned about nuclear war. As to the probability of the event, that is very difficult to estimate. I was quite worried about the 1979-1980 period (I estimated 35%), but that has passed. I now suspect that we will rise to a new peak risk in about 1984, with a drop-off after that, and a possible rise again toward the end of the decade. I suspect the change of strategic nuclear exchange over the next five years in 10-40%, and over the next ten years is 20-60%."

"As to how I act on my beliefs: I truly enjoy the isolation (of New Mexico), and so do the wife and kids. We like it where we are, but I doubt if most people would. I can step off my back porch and fire my .45 (or take a piss) and nobody can hear the report or report me to the police for indecent exposure. We lived briefly in Galveston, Texas, and Norfolk, Virginia, and for ten years in Los Angeles — actually Redondo Beach, where I ran a thirty-five-doctor multi-specialty medical clinic. We enjoyed the metro life, but we like this life better. But in all honesty, most people don't like isolation. I have seen many families come here, stay six to twelve months, and leave. My wife and I were both introduced to these mountains at an early age. We both worked as counselors and wranglers for summer camps here. We have really returned to an area and people we respect and like. I don't think most suburbanites would like it, and for them to live like we do would be a cost to pay that exceeds the risk-avoidance that is gained."

"Further (as to how I act on my beliefs), I first moved to this isolated area with no intention of tying in with the local communities. But that has changed, partly with my doing, but mostly with the doing of the community. I built my own home — designed and built mostly with my own hands: a 4,000 square foot house (including basement and solar greenhouse-collector) and barn, and miles of fence. But I recognized my boredom and the community need and have started practicing medicine again."

The physician elaborates on specific preparations: "little is specifically so geared (to nuclear survival) but if you count the aftermath, the gearing is heavy. As for fallout shelter, there is the proverbial problem of line-drawing: no matter how big or small your shelter, there will be someone you have to exclude. I try to approach difficult problems simply. Therefore, I have designed a shelter that will hold only four people (my family) and be crowded at that. That is the easiest line to draw. I have excluded my parents and siblings, and their families, because to include them moves into impossible line-drawing problems (in-laws, etc?). I have made this clear to all my relatives. I have also set up the shelter with near-perfect defensability, and they know I will defend it. After the fallout period, I will cooperate with surviving extended family and even some friends, and eventually everyone, I hope.

"With non-relative local population, I have taken a different approach. They all know that I think there my be trouble ahead. They know I think they should store food, etc. But more importantly, they all know that if things get tough, I am important to them because of my medical skills and supplies (which I also stockpile). I have also taken some other protective measures, both in the way of making us dependent on each other, and actual defensive measures. I think most of the locals would go to some length to protect me.

"The people translocated by the catastrophic event are another story. They will have taken their last shot by coming to the mountains. They have been here before to shoot deer, or drink beer, or both (or steal my horses and kill my breeder cows for the hell of it). They are my biggest threat in the aftermath of a nuclear or other disaster. I do not have total solutions to this problem. North and Hess (two survivalist writers) say I should move into the local village, but I don't want to — they arrest people for pissing off the back porch. I have taken many measures to protect myself from this threat, but it is still my weak link. Most people advocate a fortress or an isolated hideout. I have compromised on these solutions.

"Would I defend myself and my family? Yes, without hesitation. However, I know that is better to plan so as not to be put into that situation. I could well lose a battle for my life, or later a battle with the law (or more likely, the martial law kangaroo courts). I am ready, willing, able, and adequately supplied, but am planning to try hard to

avoid it. (I think many of the 'crazies' extremely militant, marauding
survivalists are looking forward to the chance.)"

The doctor's conclusion: "I don't know if I will survive a nuclear
war. But at age forty, I really am more concerned about my children
and society as a whole surviving. All I am doing is the logical steps,
based on the probable risks. I do not have a blast shelter, since this
area is not worth wasting a $2,000,000 bomb on. But the Titan missile
base in Arizona is a fallout threat. Bottom line: yes, I will survive the
bomb and fallout; I may not survive the pandemonium that follows."

There's no question, meanwhile, that some survivalists lack any
patience for community endeavors — even family commitments — at
all; they advocate an even more extreme form of "rugged individualism" instead. Some are basically just independent. They resent the intrusion of others' needs and expectations into their plans.
Others are just plain hostile to the people around them. Although it's
probably true that the stereo-type of the survivalist as misanthrope is
overworked, and that only a minority of those involved in the movement are dangerously antisocial, the fact remains that some such individuals exist.

One who follows the dictum that survival is "every man for
himself" is F.S., a young man (27) who lives in the Midwest. F.S. has
corresponded with me for several months now; we also speak long-
distance occasionally. From this exchange, I've managed to get a sense
of his concerns. They aren't lacking in contradictions. F.S. is con-
spicuously lonely, and it appears that survivalism — despite its mis-
anthropic aspects — might serve him as a foundation for possible
friendships; and yet his wariness of people is also obvious. During a
conversation in autumn of 1981, he told me, "I'm not the meek, pas-
sive kind who can just sit there and do nothing when a potential
danger threatens. An example: last year, my county was under a tornado watch in the month of June or July — I forget exactly when. The
sky got cloudy in the afternoon, and by four o'clock it was looking
pretty ugly and the conditions seemed ripe for a tornado. I went
straight home and started moving my things down into the basement,
working like a one-man stevedore gang. The whole effort took me an
hour and a half, roughly. By the end of that time the sky was almost
black, the wind blowing hard, rain just slamming down. I kept expecting the CD sirens to start blowing every moment.

"My roommate came home just as I was finishing my effort, and chided me for 'reacting without thinking things through,' or some such crap. He thought I was jumping the gun, that I should relax and not get so emotional. As he was chiding me, taking me to task for my flaws of character (or so they seemed to him) a tornado was tearing up a small town about thirty miles southwest of my home town and heading due northeast, which would have brought it right through my city had it not run out of steam. But my bunkie couldn't grasp the simple concept of taking precautions when danger might be near."

Eventually, this crisis not only broke up the friendship, but it also prompted F.S. to evaluate his priorities in general. "Perhaps this will help illustrate the difference between survivalists and non-survivalists," he said last fall. "The former takes precautions, makes plans should danger come. The latter just goes right along, blithely ignoring things until the roof caves in. Or makes a few grunts of interest. According to them, we should just sit tight, do nothing, 'don't act rashly,' and so on, until the axe falls and our heads get chopped. Well, I don't go along with that." F.S.'s skepticism intensifies when the risks involve a possible nuclear war and other catastrophes. "I won't trust a civil defense system to save me when I know the shelter setup and other facets of CD in my area are hopelessly inadequate to deal with wartime or perhaps even cataclysmic peacetime disasters like reactor meltdowns and so forth. I won't trust a government to save me when it builds a system to save the top brass but doesn't do diddly-squat for the common folks who coughed up the money to pay for that system." His conclusion: "the only one I trust to try and save is me.

"Is it bad to wish to look after your family, your loved ones, if the government doesn't seem to give a damn? No. In 1st Timothy 5:8, we find that 'He that provides not for his own and specially those of his own house has denied the faith and is worse than an infidel.' Survivalism is the ultimate in tending to your loved ones — preparing to sustain them should calamity strike."

One of the most interesting portraits of the survival movement is Bruce Clayton's *Survivalist Directory*. This book is, in fact, one of the few descriptions of more than a few individuals within the movement, and it's the only one (to my knowledge) which employs any sort of empirical method in its research. However, the absence of other studies probably says more about survivalists' reluctance to talk than it does about anyone else's willingness to listen. Members of the movement — regardless of specific beliefs or activities — generally keep quiet. Personel security is a common obsession among survivalists. As a result, even the existence of Clayton's *Directory* is remarkable; and its sociological importance is mostly a side effect of other purposes.

The *Directory* is "a book and a service which provides for secure, two-way letter exchanges between survivalists." Clayton, a prominent writer within the survival movement, designed this service "to help survivalists who wish to get in touch with people of similar interest without compromising anyone's anonymity or security." In short, it's "rather like computer dating (your shelter or mine?)" according to one advertisement. Clayton also states that "one of my primary motives in going to the trouble to set up this service was to find out who the survivalists really are. There are a lot of elaborate myths in the field, particularly where the news media are involved, so I thought it might be a service to collect 150+ survivalists and let them speak for themselves."

Clayton admits that the *Directory* questionnaire "was not designed as a statistical survey form, but rather as a prompting device to encourage respondents to tell us their thoughts in their own words." He also suggests that his own reputation as an advocate of nuclear survivalism may have affected some of the response. Persons who answered Clayton's questionnaire sought him out voluntarily; this type of "self-selected" sample most often produces different results from those in a random selection. Still, the *Directory* write-ups are interesting. They provide the best overview of survivalists to date.

Examining the results, Clayton makes the following generalizations:

Sex. "Most of the respondents seem to be male heads of households. There are a number of single males but they do not predominate. I'd say 10% or less of the questionnaires were from females."

Age. "Ages range from late teens into the 70's and 80's. Many respondents seem to be in their early thirties but there is no clear age class involved."

Race. "Respondents were predominately Caucasian. However, a few Negro, Eurasian, Latin American, Amerind, and mixed-race survivalists also responded."

Religion. "There didn't seem to be any trend in terms of religion. Christians (of many varieties) predominated, but Born-Again

Christians, Mormons, Jews, Agnostics, Atheists, and people who were simply not interested in religion were well represented, too." Clayton also notes that "there were surprisingly few Mormons, considering the relatively large number of Mormon survivalists. I surmise that their church social structure fulfills their need to find others of similar interests." His conclusion: "most of the respondents in the **Directory** tend to be isolated survivalists in search of others."

Political affiliation. "There was a definite trend in terms of politics, but not quite in the way one might guess. Survivalists have a media reputation for being ultra-conservatives." Clayton, however, notes that "In contrast, the current breakdown of Directory respondents is: Independent (32), Conservative (20), Libertarian (18), Right (15), Republican (11), Moderate (3), Ultra-conservative (3), Democrats (2), Left (1), Liberal (1), Radical (1). Clayton's observations: "the streak of independence, of active dislike for the more traditional political parties is quite evident (even at the liberal end of the scale). So is the general trend to the right of center, but not far to the right." He also mentions that one interesting aspect of the sample "was the number of people who identified themselves as being 'conservative' or to the 'right' but who did not want to hear from 'right-wing nuts.' "

Education. In this regard, Clayton states that "There did not seem to be any particular correlation between education and survivalist attitudes. The education of the respondents in this sample ranged from six years of formal schooling to the Ph.D. and M.D. level." He specifies that "several respondents were members of Mensa, the high-IQ society," that "many people had an impressive array of VoTech certificates and experience in blue-collar skills," and that "overall, there was a striking sense of diversity in skills and training, as in the case of the chemical engineer who was also a college science professor, a computer programmer, and a lawyer."

This analysis of data, though superficial and admittedly based on a sample of uncertain significance, nonetheless gives some idea of trends within the survival movement. If nothing else, it serves to dispel the stereotype that all survivalists are semiliterate, politically extreme hermits. The movement appears to be more diverse than most observers acknowledge. Other trends exist, too, but for the most part they concern issues other than race, religion, or politics in general. (Subsequent chapters of this book will examine some of these issues in detail.)

Clayton's own generalizations are that "Most survivalists are not rich dilettantes. Most are not uneducated rednecks. Most are not hate-filled racists, although they are conscious of racial distinctions. Most are not panicky alarmists. Most are not trigger-happy sadists." He concedes that "There are a few of each of these groups represented here," but he claims that "the overall picture is of responsible people with confidence in their own foresight, who are trying to come to grips with threats that their government is ignoring...or creating, depending on your point of view." Although these opinions may include some which reflect Clayton's commitment to survivalism, his conclusion is perhaps more objective: "After preparing these biographies I would characterize survivalists as people who have a strong streak of independence, self-confidence, and optimism. Why optimism? How else would you describe someone who believes he can cope with a nuclear attack?" He adds, "That's about as optimistic as a person can get."

This brings us to the next question: what do survivalists think of nuclear war? Of its likelihood? Of its consequences? Of the responses they make to it? Survivalists in Clayton's *Directory* give only brief remarks of their beliefs. Still — as often seems the case — the *Directory* gives a revealing glimpse into hopes, fears, and intentions.

Of the 161 respondents, 58 make some sort of explicit reference to the possibility of nuclear war. Another 39 refer to nuclear war in a more implicit manner. (All references to individual survivalists in the *Directory* employ the state-plus-number codes which Clayton uses for maintaining anonymity: AL1, FL4, OH3, etc.) As regards the explicit / implicit distinction, I'm considering a comment like CA19's — "I concluded several years ago...that conflict and nuclear exchange with the Soviet Union was probably inevitable" — to be explicit. On the other hand, a reference to nuclear preparedness without direct mention of war implies the concern anyway: "Currently working with the local Civil Defense Dept.; radiological monitor/shelter manager," for example, as OH8 indicates. In addition, six respondents remark on worries or activities which seem difficult to interpret. Some of these suggest general concerns about military weakness; one specifies a worry about conventional warfare. The result is that 102 respondents in the *Directory* express one or another degree of concern about prospects for a nuclear war.

It is important to note that not all survivalists have a clear sense of what they expect to happen. Their sense of dread is intense;

however, some of them hesitate to make crystal-ball predictions. For instance, CA37 states that "I'm expecting a calamity to strike mankind," but he adds, "I don't pretend to know what this may be. It could be as simple as an intensification of the problems we are already confronting or the third world war, or economic collapse, etc." AZ1 sees some connections between possible disasters; he is "mainly worried about nuclear war," but he's also concerned about "an economic collapse which... would lead to war." CO4 is even more explicit. He is concerned about "socio-economic collapse in the U.S.... run-away government control of masses and depletion of individual freedoms leading to revolt of the masses... building global pressures bringing about sure war in the Mideast leading to limited surgical confrontation between US/USSR..." Many survivalists feel that these problems — whether sudden or gradual, separate or cumulative — will have drastic effects on western culture. "I concluded several years ago (circa 1974)," says CA19, "that conflict and nuclear exchange with the Soviet Union was probably inevitable. This combined with multiple other insoluable (sic) problems, both domestic and international, will probably signal the end of civilization as we have known it."

Some survivalists specify events and timing in more detail. AZ2, for example, says that "(I) foresee nuclear war in 85-86; worse than that beginning 1990." Similarly, WV1 states that "For approximately ten years I have been concerned about the possibility of nuclear war.. .I now believe that such an event is inevitable and believe that the most likely time span for this to occur would be between 1/1/84 and 12/31/85/." Although most survivalists' expectations aren't beyond possibility — and at times more likely than even non-survivalists would care to admit — some of their scenarios are implausible, even silly. FL6 expects to see "a large part of Florida, the Gulf of Mexico states and the western U.S. and Alaska being invaded by Russians from the north via the AlCan Highway, Cubans across the straights (sic) of Florida and leftist guerillas (sic) from Nicaragua and El Salvador coming up the Pan American Highway via Mexico." All these groups, he says, "will be using neutron warheads and poison gas (as in Laos and Afganistan) to put down any opposition. Occupation will be very long and brutal." Likewise, some respondents in the Directory base their interpretations less on political trends than on religious faith. OH8 states that "I believe the predictions in the Bible will come to pass. Russia will not attack us; it will be a United States of Europe led by Germany." FL3, much in the same vein, worries about nuclear war, one-world government, and "the rise of the antichrist."

In short, survivalists' concerns vary considerably — from well-grounded political speculation to outlandish paranoia — and even those which focus on nuclear war do so for many different reasons. What seems consistent is a general response toward threats regardless of whether the threats are real or imagined. Survivalists feel, as Emerson put it, that "things are in the saddle and riding Man." They resent their helplessness. They intend to do something about it. Clayton's *Directory* gives a clear sense of this intention: to take hold of their fate again.

MT1 writes that "I am not looking forward to economic chaos, nuclear war, etc., but I am realistic (I hope) about today's world. It's better to be protected than worry." Similarly, CA38 explains his decision to become a survivalist: "I guess that if we don't take care of ourselves, no one else will do it for us." Some survivalists reach a realization because of a particular experience. CA26 explored the current U.S. civil defense program and came away even more worried than he was before. "We have nothing. Plan nothing," he states in the *Directory*. "The U.S. government has no plans to instruct the population in nuclear survival. The only government plan is to relocate the population out of big cities. This looks like a sure disaster." His decision is "that I should do something about survival." Most survivalists would agree that he should, that they themselves should, that everyone should. Uncertain about the chances for collective efforts, they consequently undertake the project alone or with a few family members and friends.

A few survivalists make their efforts not just for material well-being, but for psychological reasons as well. According to NC4, "I am convinced that a nuclear attack on America is inevitable. My question is not if but when. This conviction is so strong that I am compelled to prepare. To do otherwise would entail a loss of self-respect and peace of mind." IA1 sums up the survivalists reasoning as tersely as anyone: "with the increased spread of nuclear arms and the apparent inability of man to prevent war we see the use of nuclear war as inevitable and would rather live than become a statistic. Survival preparation gives us a form of security in a world situation where we have little control."

Security in a world where we have little control.

If any one can sum up the survival movement, this is it. Other people resent their helplessness, of course; the survivalists have no monopoly on frustration, anxiety, or even a sense of impending doom.

Where these people differ from non-survivalists is in taking certain specific steps to overcome their sense of helplessness and to replace it with some sort of security instead.

What are these steps? Are they effective? Is it possible that the survivalists will somehow make it through a nuclear catastrophe in which everyone else (or almost everyone) will succumb? Or is it more likely that these steps will prove inadequate, and the sense of security resulting from them will foster nothing but illusions? What if the survivalists are kidding themselves?

These questions have prompted this book, and each of the following chapters will approach the answers in one way or another. The issues are complexly interrelated; however, the task of examining them requires at least some effort at separating one from another — otherwise it's all too easy to get tangled up in everything at once. I have therefore marked off what seem to be the most important issues within the survival movement, and I examine each of them separately before considering their interactions.

Survival theory, for instance, forms the basis from which many survivalists take action. Why should you try to survive? And *what* are you surviving? How should you go about doing it? Various writers and "survival consultants" have become prominent theoreticians — a kind of brain trust — within the movement, and they influence the beliefs and behavior of thousands of rank and file survivalists. What some of these theoriticians advocate warrant special analysis. Since food, shelter and personal defense are consistently among their greatest concerns, subsequent chapters examine each of these subjects. A later chapter explores the related issue of civil defense — a form of nuclear preparedness which both resembles and differs from survivalism. The final chapters consider the most crucial matter: will even massive preparation make it possible to survive a nuclear war?

Before proceeding, however, I would like to offer one final portrait of an individual survivalist. Some members of the movement embody the obsessiveness — even fanaticism — which has caught so much attention from the popular media; others show signs of a more multi-dimensional personality. I mention this not to exempt survivalists from criticism, but rather to suggest that certain individuals at least struggle with complex ethical problems. Whether they succeed in reaching satisfactory resolution seems questionable, but the effort is certainly there. Some survivalists find their own activities both compelling and worrisome.

N.R. is one of them. Thirty-one years of age, he has been a sur-vivalist for most of his adult life, yet he remains ambivalent about the movement, his participation in it, and its potential consequences. I've transcribed the following interview verbatim to retain a sense of N.R.'s varied thoughts on survivalism.

Q: What are your concerns as a survivalist?

A: Nuclear is one of the areas I'm most concerned with. *The* most concerned with. Also, if you satisfy the requirements for dealing with nuclear survival, you either define the parameters of survival for other situations, or you take care of them. There's an ongoing problem with nuclear war. You can't put the genie back in the bottle. Once it is unleashed — the potential for using the weapon — the risk is there.

Q: What do you foresee happening?

A: I suppose at one time I was very concerned about a tight scenario — particular events. Now it's more general. The major urgency is the Soviet threat. I see the major balancing force as China. But so many countries are getting involved with nuclear development. France helping Saudi Arabia... There's an ever-growing activity of this sort in the world.

Q: But you expect a Soviet attack?

A: I do, especially in the next ten years. It would be imperative, if the Soviets were pursuing nuclear war, to knock out missile bases and command centers — at least.

Q: What does this mean for your own survival?

A: I feel real uncomfortable living here (a major American city). The metro areas would be a real dangerous area for fallout. I definitely find myself on the side of feeling there should be some nuclear preparedness, both public and private.

Q: So what plans do you have?

A: To leave this area. I've already attempted to relocate — I tried to relocate in the Northwest, but I found it too cold. There are some other places I like better. I've visited one several times. I know the state pretty well. Since I live at a reasonable distance from it, this is something I can explore easily. I'll try to work things out according to my work. I'd have to make some lifestyle changes. But regarding general attitudes: I was of the opinion that I needed to be very much removed from large population areas. But I would now rather be living in a city than in a rural area. The fact that there are no target areas nearby — I like cities, what's available, the diversity. I do think if I'd grown up in a rural area, I would be better able to adjust. But I can't expect myself to change those underlying preferences.

Q: So it's a matter of making the changes you can without disrupting your whole life.

A: Right.

Q: What are your feelings about trying to survive where you are now?

A: Having read the materials I've read, and knowing what I know, I could increase my chances of surviving significantly.

Q: Specifically? Do you have a shelter? Have you stored food? And so forth.

A: I don't have a blast shelter. I don't have a fallout shelter. I do have food stored. Also, I have an awareness of where the fallout shelters are in the area. I'd be one of the people who spontaneously evacuates during a crisis. Although I have no specific idea about where to go, I'd be better off than people who stayed. This is a coalescing picture.

Q: Tell me something about your history as a survivalist. How did you get interested, who influenced you, how has the interest developed?

A: It probably started with — and this was way back — reading *Atlas Shrugged*, by Ayn Rand. This was when I was in high school. This led me to a number of various authors. I read Harry Browne's

You Can Profit from a Monetary Crisis... Mostly he deals with economic and financial issues. Then I got involved with a group of enthusiasts of Ayn Rand. This was around 1974-76. Then my interest in retreating got focused. I bought my own property, (near where N.R. now lives) and was making plans to make this my own retreat. I had a little place up in the hills and was stocking it up. It was a long drive, though, and I wasn't spending as much time there as I wanted. This situation was me — on my own — thinking of inviting family or friends, etc., along if things got bad.

Then I had a change of thought: you're going to have to have a retreat right there where you are. I'd actually like to live where the retreat is. This was part of the process of being part of a group.

Q: You joined a survival group?

A: Yes.

Q: Could you tell me more about it?

A: I went to a meeting. At the time, I was scouting out prospects for a group. I was enthusiastic about this particular group. What happened was that I got interested in a fellow who was setting up a retreat in the Northwest. The problem was whether I could find a job there. Then I got a job offer. Later that year — this was summer of '79 — I moved up, tried the job, didn't like it, changed, found a place to live. I bought a house and stocked it. (I'm willing to take action even though it makes me look like a fool. Later, I regretted buying that house — I've had trouble selling it. But this sort of thing has given me lots of insight into the dynamics of stages I go through psychologically in a crisis. I think this sort of insight could help me survive.)

Q: Tell me more about the group.

A: It was small — twelve to fifteen members. There were peripheral people and a core group. There got to be ins and outs. It got to be very uncomfortable how the group developed.

Q: What happened?

A: One of the things that motivated me to join a group was the need to have a community. There were some very strong personalities in this group. Some of them had read *Atlas Shrugged*, and so forth... In part, it was a family group — it had family members which organizers had tried to draw in. I got very involved... I was considered to be one of the five or six core group members. I was involved with planning. But that evolved and changed quickly — and ended in a situation where they suggested that they were concerned about how heavily I was leaning on them. Others in the group were residents — had lived in the area five or six years. Others were not located physically as close by — this is one thing which made them peripheral members. But the core members felt I was too dependent on them.

Q: Socially?

A: That was part of it.

Q: So they wanted you to be involved, but they also wanted you to have your own life elsewhere.

A: I suppose.

Q: And that caused some of the stress?

A: There were some heavy dynamics. One member thought of herself as very psychological and aware of group dynamics... Actually, I visited Twin Oaks (a group community) in Virginia, and I read a book about the place after leaving the Northwest. There were lots of correlations. All these groups — back-to-the-land, religious, any groups following a plan or direction — always go through these dynamics and interactions. It was exhausting and draining.

Q: And so the pressure kept building?

A: I found the group concept very difficult. It was hard to reach any agreement on how to take action. Secrecy was a problem. I actually found myself becoming paranoid. When I'm involved in a group, I may feel I'm acting appropriately, but other members may feel I'm not. It ended up a bad experience. The instigators were expressing that I was losing my balance. They suggested that I see a psychiatrist.

I did that. Basically, I found a very sympathetic ear. He said maybe the group isn't what you need — I was restricting myself too severely. This was very good advice.

One of the mind-boggling pressures was — Shit! If it's like this *now*, what's it going to be like during a nuclear war? I was convinced that the world was falling apart. This was during the Iranian crisis of 1979-80. The external pressure contributed to my problems. But the actual stress of a nuclear war sure wouldn't be any less.

Q: I'm curious about some specific aspects of the group. Could you tell me more about what the people planned, what they did? What were their backgrounds?

A: The leader was a professional designer, but did some work with writing — sort of a dual profession. He was in his late thirties to early forties. Then there was another couple — professionals — also thirty-five to forty. Then there was a younger couple, around twenty-eight or -nine. He was in construction; she was a nurse. There was also that psychological lady. She was working on her Ph.D. or something. Other couples got involved later. After my problems with relocating, the group decided to recruit more locally — family type with kids. Very few of us were single. The group attitude was that singles were destabilizing.

Q: What about plans? Was there an actual retreat?

A: This was one of the most disquieting aspects. I had assumed that there was an actual site being developed. As I looked back later, I tried to find what had indicated this. I realized that it wasn't so. The group was just trying to balance out personalities first.

Q: There wasn't any retreat at all?

A: No. I might have been better to have one person buying land, organizing, and deciding who got in.

Q: So you ended up leaving.

A: Thing didn't work out very well. The group wasn't what it was supposed to be.

Q: Something else I'm curious about: the whole weapons issue.

A: Everybody owned weapons. This was considered part of everybody's responsibility — to be part of this. There was a lot of discussion about contingency plans: what if a woman with a child comes to the door wanting food? We tried to deal with this. The consensus was that we were an exclusion group. We would maintain our exclusivity — by force, if necessary.

Q: What was your attitude about this?

A: I don't have that sort of awareness. I have purchased weapons and have become proficient with them. But it's hard for me to envision myself pulling the trigger on a gun. One of the things that made me uncomfortable was the pressure of feeling that the group wanted me to decide that issue right now. So I thought: maybe it would be better for me to duck out now.

Q: There was pressure on you to decide exactly where you stood — the woman-with-child issue, for instance?

A: Yes. There was some pressure to feel, "In 100% of occasions, I will pull the trigger." It was a criterion for being in the group. It was sort of deciding — subconsciously, or below the up-front level — that people should say, "We have a consistant line. We want to know how you will respond." It was sort of the unspoken criterion for being a member of the group, and especially the core group. They needed to come to terms with this — wanted to defend the retreat under any threat. I suppose it makes sense that a group must have a known limit.

Q: But did you feel pressured?

A: I felt sort of bullied into it. Not at the time. But in retrospect, I felt bullied into it. The thing I particularly thought about was: are particular people a threat? If I were confronting an armed person who said, "Drop your gun!" I wouldn't have a problem with that (using weapons). The moral problem is meeting someone halfway who is harmless and unarmed. But what if the mother and child were just reconaissance for a group of looters? — the group asked. It got real crazy. I got real uncomfortable after a while. I didn't see these as the most important issues for the group.

Q: So what are you plans now?

A: I consider the best survival group to be the family. The individual is working at a disadvantage. You might be able to work on an individual basis and survive, but one important aspect is to be in a community where people won't be stuck in fallout shelters for two months. In the place I'm going to, I could emerge in about a week. I expect larger communities to work and deal with issues of survival better than individuals can. I'd like to live within a city. A community can coalesce. Even if people haven't provided for survival, the community itself won't be totally ravaged. There will be enough pressure knowing that there's total destruction 100-150 miles away.

Chapter Two

Survivalist Theoreticians

As in other social trends, various factions have arisen within the survival movement, each with its own tenets, goals, methods, and style. There may be more unaffiliated "members" in this movement, however, than in others, because of survivalists' reticence. And yet certain individuals are less reticent than others, and some even appear to be leaders. Among them are a few who are survivalist theoreticians. These are people who either express what is already popular wisdom among a particular group of survivalists, or else they formulate ideas, strategy, or technology which others then adopt. The most prominent of these theotreticians are Bruce Clayton, Cresson Kearny, and Kurt Saxon.

A relative newcomer to survivalism who is increasingly influential within the movement is Bruce Clayton. A plant ecologist by training, he became concerned about nuclear war several years ago, studied the risks and possible consequences "in a spirit of scientific curiosity," and concluded that many popular assumptions were mistaken. His chief contribution to the movement since then has been to argue against what he calls "doomie fantasies" and to replace them with more accurate information. Clayton's recent book, *Life After Doomsday*, argues against the common belief that nuclear war would annihilate humankind, and it claims instead that "with careful preparation, any family or small group of people can insure its own survival." The book also provides detailed analysis of nuclear warfare and outlines the courses of action which people can take in response to it. In addition, Clayton writes for a variety of survivalist publications, including *Survive*, the first national magazine devoted entirely to the movement; and he has recently developed the *Survivalist Directory* a book "designed to put survivalists in contact with other survivalists." This directory is an especially significant development, for it may provide more of a survivalist network than has existed previously.

Clayton describes himself as "a prominent second-stringer aspiring to become first string" among survivalist theoreticians, but his influence may well go beyond this assessment. The reason is that Clayton is the first writer to legitimate what many people regard as "hard-core" survivalism. (He and others have objected to the hard-core/soft-core distinction, and perhaps rightly so. The survival movement does, in fact, appear to be more complex than what these labels would suggest. Clayton himself has developed an alternate scheme which identifies the various factions more accurately than does a mere dichotomy of hard and soft.) Until the publication of *Life After Doomsday*, most survivalists with any public visibility tended either to be followers of Howard Ruff get-rich-during-hard-times school, or else they were isolated and often militant eccentrics. Other factions existed, but they kept a low profile. Those advocating rural retreats, for instance, said little or nothing about their preparations. To some extent, this is still true. What has changed is that *Doomsday* (as Clayton calls it) and a few other books have made serious survivalism more respectable.

Clayton's educational background accounts for some of his reputation. As a professional scientist, Clayton writes more convincingly about nuclear war than do most other survivalist writers, and his training gives him an air of authority when he interprets the possible consequences. Whether such credentials are sufficient is another matter; and whether his information is right or wrong is still another. But the fact remains that Clayton — as well as some of his trained colleagues — cannot be dismissed as kooks or charlatans. Even a brief conversation with him makes it clear that he is intelligent, articulate, and concerned. He has done extensive research on many topics pertinent to survivalism; he has thought through at least some of their implications; and thus any attempt to accept or refute his conclusions must begin by acknowledging, not dismissing, his education.

The argument given in *Life After Doomsday* is fairly simple: "For most Americans," Clayton writes, "survival of at least the first few weeks following a nuclear attack is not only possible, it is almost unavoidable." This goes against almost all common knowledge, of course: who could possibly survive a nuclear war? If the blast doesn't kill you, then won't the radiation? Clayton states otherwise. Although he admits that a nuclear war would be "the greatest social and biological catastrophe our world has ever known," he argues that even a massive exchange of weapon fire between the United States and the Soviet Union would produce far less drastic effects than people imagine. It would not be the end of the human race or even of civilization.

Do these claims hold up under scrutiny? The answer is too complex to provide here. My point right now is simply that Clayton regards most popular images of nuclear war as simplistic and exaggerated. He offers an alternative view, and backs it up with evidence from several technical studies. Many people find this view persuasive. The implication for Clayton and for some of his readers, at least, is clear: if nuclear war isn't the utter end-all that many of us have assumed, then people must be ready for its aftermath.

Life After Doomsday therefore provides information for nuclear survival. Chapters cover subjects such as evacuation, shelter, food, emergency medicine, personal defense, and general strategy. Appendices discuss target areas within the United States, expedient construction of shelters, and a variety of other technical matter. The book ends with an earnest "Good luck." And drastic as all this may sound, Clayton regards the agenda as essentially optimistic. "I feel that the 'survival' message is a much more useful approach to educating people about the dangers of nuclear war than the 'disarm or die' approach," he says, "because it is positive and hopeful."

Cresson Kearny is also an optimistic survivalist writer; and like Clayton, he bases his optimism on technical data and a be-prepared strategy. Kearny's background — both theoretical and practical — is more extensive than Clayton's. His work as an engineer and inventor at the Oak Ridge National Laboratory (1964 through 1979) produced a variety of survival plans and devices which many survivalists have adopted. During those years, however, Kearny became so angry about U.S. government policies — in particular, the nuclear strategy called "Mutually Assured Destruction" — that he resigned from the laboratory to promote his ideas without conflict of interest. The result was the book *Nuclear War Survival Skills*, a compendium of plans for "expedient shelter and homemade life-support equipment" — and probably the most complete manual of its sort available in the United States today.

Nuclear War Survival Skills covers most of the same topics as those in *Life After Doomsday*, but in greater detail. (The chief exception is personal defense; which Kearny regards as unnecessary.) Since Kearny's work at Oak Ridge emphasized engineering and testing of various shelter designs and pieces of survival equipment, his emphasis is almost entirely technical. There is, however, some initial space provided for general theory. This stresses Kearny's belief that a disparity between U.S. and Soviet nuclear policies makes war not only probably, but potentially more catastrophic to Americans than to Russians.

> No nation other than the United States has advocated or adopted a strategy that purposely leaves its citizens unprotected hostages to its enemies. The rulers of the Soviet Union continue to prepare the Russians to fight, survive, and win a nuclear war. In contrast, influential Americans continue to demoralize us with exaggerated descriptions of nuclear war.

Kearny would perhaps reject the label of survivalist for himself. His background certainly emphasizes a commitment to civil defense, and the differences between the two orientations are significant. Civil defense differs from survivalism much as mass transit differs from individual ownership of cars. Recent statements suggest that Kearny still prefers civil defense projects of national scope to the alternatives. "I view the new interest in civil defense by Reagan's people as a most hopeful sign," he told me. But he regards mere interest as inadequate, and he went on to say that "If the government doesn't take measures for civil defense, then individuals should." This is where the public orientation flows into private efforts. Kearny therefore urges individuals to undertake what their leaders have neglected, and he offers *Nuclear War Survival Skills* as a partial means to that end.

One writer who is controversial not only outside of survivalist circles, but inside them as well, is Kurt Saxon. A former newspaperman, Saxon is the author of *The Poor Man's James Bond* (a do-it-yourself weapons manual) and a strident newsletter called *The Survivor*. His slant is not simply that World War III wouldn't be so bad, but that it "will be a blessing for the survivors. We can start anew, hopefully avoiding past errors." He goes on to say that "the earth's surplus population is long overdue for a culling," and that "America has terminal cancer. A cancer cell is a cell that consumes resources, serves no useful purpose and multiplies, and we have a hell of a lot of cancer cells. We're importing them from Mexico, from Cuba, who knows how many Haitians and Orientals, all cancer cells, and we don't need them."

Saxon's intent is therefore to provide information and advice to non-cancerous Americans — presumably WASPs — for the purpose of fostering their survival. His company, Atlan Formularies, offers books to survivalists on a typical range of subjects: nuclear war survival, self-defense, and food storage. *The Survivor*, a monthly periodical, elaborates on these subjects and advocates a mixture of back-to-the-land self-sufficiency and 19th century mechanical know-how. The upshot of Saxon's agenda is a Social Darwinist utopia:

> Following the collapse and/or nuclear war, there will be up to three billion less humans to share our planet with.... After the initial chaos it may take up to five years for the roots of civilization to send up shoots. Citizens of small towns will immediately organize to fight off bands of refugees and marauders. City and suburban survivors will scrounge from the rubble enough to barely live. Finally, after the less adaptable have died out, the criminal elements have been killed off, and the survivors have become more interested in trading with than killing one another, culture will reemerge.

Whatever Saxon's opinions, and whatever people's criticism of him, the fact remains that he is one of the most influential survivalists — at least among certain factions. Some of this influence is a result of his own quest for recognition (I love publicity,   he told me); some is also a consequence of his cultural biases ("I'm called a racist, but I've never said blacks are the only people you should be afraid of"). Some influence, too, is the side-effect of other people's frustrations. He says, "People have given up hope for the establishment, and we must take matters into our own hands." Much of Saxon's appeal is that he encourages his followers to do just that.

Other survivalist theoreticians are not as well-known as Clayton, Kearny, or Saxon, but are influential within certain circles. They may be prominent within a limited geographical area, for instance; or they may have followers within a particular subculture. Typical of these theoreticians are T.F. Nieman, Duncan Long, and Jim McKeever.

One theoretician whose interests have a specific focus is Thomas F. Nieman, whose thirty-five years of business experience includes the manufacture of survival tents. Nieman has recently published a manual on fallout — blast-shelters called *Better "Read" Than Dead: The Complete Book of Nuclear Survival*. Nieman acknowledges that other books cover the same material, but states that "I've added more detail in a simple language than the others, so that the average person can understand it." Like other survivalists, he believes that "You can survive, but it's going to take many systems of defensive knowledge in order to do it. The people of this country *must* have this knowledge."

Nieman's book contains information on target areas, fallout "hot spots," radiation effects, survival planning, and shelter, among other topics. Generally speaking, it lives up to the author's claims of intelligibility. The thesis, as in Clayton's in *Life After Doomsday*, is that many people can survive a nuclear war if properly prepared, and they should therefore prepare as fully as possible. Unlike the others, however, Nieman seems less concerned with possible Soviet attack on the United States than with a variety of disasters. He told me, "Nobody is going to blast us off the face of the earth. The Russians don't want war." Then what is he concerned about? "I'm more worried about terrorist groups."

Duncan Long, meanwhile, is another writer whose skepticism about surviving a nuclear war turned into confidence that it's possible, even easy, with the right preparation. "I was flabberghasted when I found out the reality of nuclear war," he said in a recent interview. "Then I decided to *do* something about it — something that would help others — and so I wrote a book." The book, *Nuclear War Sur-*

vival, is like most survivalist manuals. It begins with warnings against inaction, proceeds to explanations of nuclear war, and then offers recommendations about how to deal with the consequences. Most of the information is succinct — even simplistic. In addition, Long offers all sorts of "keep your chin up" encouragement: "survival wouldn't be easy...but it would be impossible.... Don't give up. The things you now own don't mean happiness. But living each day to the fullest, having faith in God, protecting your family and enjoying just being alive — these things are truly important and bring true happiness."

Another theoretician with a cheery outlook for nuclear war is Jim McKeever. His book, *Christians Will Go through the Tribulation.. .And How to Prepare for It*, is a manual for those who believe that a period of catastrophe, long since predicted in the Bible now awaits us. It starts with an interpretation of the Book of Revelation and proceeds to advise Christians how they can brace themselves for the Tribulation — seven years of hard times that will precede the Second Coming. According to McKeever, the Tribulation will begin with a thermonuclear war. Not all is lost however:

> The doomsday people say if a nuclear war hits, humanity will be nearly wiped out, and then they won't want to be alive. I believe that such people are not speaking words of truth from God. *Many* people will survive.... In a time of chaos like that, people are much more open to turning to God. I believe that it is the duty of every Christian to do everything he can to stay alive so that he can share the good news Gospel with the victims of the nuclear war.

And the Tribulation — including the war which begins it — serves an important purpose in McKeever's understanding of the future.

> A major purpose of the Tribulation...is to destroy all of the evil and unrighteousness on the earth... After this purging and purifying of the earth, nature will be set free; the wolves and the sheep will be able to live in harmony with each other, and Christ will reign over a revised planet earth.

This in turn gives rise to McKeever's intense optimism.

Evidently God wants Christians here on earth during this process of purification of the earth. This must mean that He wants to use us in the process. I find that really exciting!... Not only do I believe that I will be here to go through it; I am really looking forward to it.

Much of this is fairly standard fundamentalist doomsaying, of course. Where McKeever parts company with some of his fellow preachers, though, is in advocating a variety of practical measures for his followers to take while they wait. These include the preparations to become more self-sufficient; to move into rural areas; and to survive famine, earthquakes, and nuclear war. In short, McKeever recommends what many other survivalists do also, but his advice is cloaked in Christian eschatology.

Along with warnings of impending disasters, God is telling His people *how* to prepare. That, of course, is one of the purposes of this book: to bring together many of the major things that God is saying to His people, both about physical and spiritual preparation for the Tribulation.

What will happen to the Christians who do not heed God's warnings and prepare? I do not know. I feel in my spirit that they will severely regret not having listened to God. Just as in the case of Noah or Joseph, I am not sure that God is under an obligation to take care of an individual who does not heed His warnings.

Three other theoreticians warrant at least a brief mention:mel and Nancy Tappan, and Howard Ruff. The Tappans are not primarily concerned with nuclear survivalism, but their influence within the survivalist community makes them significant in general. As for Ruff, many people — including Ruff himself — would question whether he is a survivalist at all; again, what seems pertinent right now isn't any particular label, but rather the man's effect on the movement itself.

Mel Tappan was one of founders of modern survivalism. Although influenced by writers as disparate as Paul Ehrlich (*The Population Bomb*) and Ayn Rand (*Atlas Shrugged*), Tappan grew interested in survivalism through his work as a corporate finance executive and investment counselor. He was concerned during the mid-1970's that the United States would soon experience fiscal collapse.

One crisis might easily lead to another, he theorized, and so he and his wife moved to Oregon, where they worked to achieve as much self-sufficiency as possible. Mel Tappan soon became a leading survivalist writer, particulary regarding personal defense. Writing in *Tappan on Survival*, he stated:

> Two years ago I would have said that war...was the least likely of the three primary scenarios (socio-economic collapse, dictatorship, or war). After all, why wouldn't the Soviets merely outlast us?...
>
> That logic no longer obtains, however. The Soviet economy is presently in even worse condition than our own, and by 1982 the Russians will be net importers of oil. Internally, their condition is desperate — and a new element has been added. They now have contempt for U.S. willingness to protect its own vital interests, and that attitude, coupled with their pressing need for oil, may well lead to further adventurism and a serious confrontation which neither side wants.

This and Mel Tappan's other concerns prompted him to recommend a program of personal survival preparation which would cover all eventualities, including nuclear war. Through his books *Survival Guns* and *Tappan on Survival*, he outlined ways for people to make such preparations. In addition, *Personal Survival Letter*, which he published with his wife, Nancy, provided a forum for prominent survivalist writers to offer other kinds of advice.

Nancy Tappan has continued *PSL* since her husband's death in 1980. Her own interests overlap considerably with Mel's, but her style is more easy-going — in some ways indistinguishable from many followers of the "back-to-the-land" movement. "It's very basic and simple," she explained recently. "It's just returning to how we used to live forty or fifty years ago." She considers basic technology and living off her small Oregon farm to be her main concerns. Regarding nuclear war, she says, "I don't know a great deal about it — I really don't have very strong opinions." At the same time, she admits that "I'm in the safest place I can be," considering likely target and fallout areas. She implies that her remaining there after her husband's death was not only accidental, as her activities are still consistently oriented toward survivalism. Editing and publishing the *Personal Survival Letter*, which is influential beyond the limits of its narrow circulation, makes Nancy Tappan one of the prominent survivalist spokespersons in the United States.

Howard Ruff, meanwhile, is a theoretician who seems a kind of borderline survivalist. His *How to Prosper During the Coming Bad Years*, a "crash course in personal and financial survival" became a bestseller in 1979. It is essentially an investment manual. However, many of Ruff's recommendations follow what might be called the "basic" survivalist agenda: 1)get out of the big urban centers; 2) avoid debt; 3)invest in silver and gold; 4) prepare for price controls and worsening inflation; and, 5) store a year's supply of food. Ruff is, in fact, generally considered one of the leaders of the movement's "soft-core" followers, and he cultivates that image. Regarding nuclear war, Ruff is somewhat defensive:

> I don't know how to prepare for the end of the world, so I'm not even going to try.... I think that we should simply prepare prudently for the worst possible case for which practical preparations are possible.... I am not going to set up a retreat and plan to "shoot the starving hordes"if they come after me.

Ruff's greatest significance for survivalism — whether nuclear or not — may be that he serves to introduce many people to a movement which they might otherwise ignore.

Although the above summary mentions fewer than ten survivalist writers, and though others may be important in some respects, these are currently the most influential among those concerned with nuclear war. They are also characteristic of the largest factions within the survivalist movement. Viewing them collectively gives a sense of the variety of backgroud, personality, belief, activity, and goal among survivalists generally. At the same time, certain themes recur in what these people have to say. Since these themes suggest some basic concerns, they warrant closer attention.

The most obvious opinion is a fear that a nuclear war will befall us soon. Individuals differ on what else may occur, and with what effects — the most common events include economic collapse; natural disasters; depletion or restriction of resources, especially in the form of oil embargoes; and tyrannical government as a consequence of one or more other crises — but the greatest overiding fear is still nuclear war. Some survivalist writers anticipate one or more initial crises leading to the final one: an oil embargo, for instance, might precipitate nuclear war. None states exactly what he expects or when.

Each of these writers expresses concern about the risk of nuclear war in various degrees of intensity. Cresson Kearny is the most reluctant to predict the future: "i have no crystal ball," he declared when asked about the likelihood of a war, "but the chances are high enough to justify effort in preparation." In contrast, Bruce Clayton hedges his bets and considers it "one of those paradoxical situations where the event is, oddly, both unlikely *and* certain to happen sooner or later." Meanwhile, Jim McKeever regards it as imminent, since "There is a high probability that we are living in the last days" — and, by implication within his scheme of things, near the start of a nuclear war. And Kurt Saxon offer an opinion without any hesitation: "in the next two years I see the collapse of organized societies worldwide, due mainly to the cutoff of Mideast oil, probably resulting in nuclear war."

There's more consensus on how to deal with the danger. Regardless of what they figure will happen, these survivalist writers advocate getting ready for it. Hope that everything will work out all right, or that somehow the world will muddle through, is not an opinion which often appears. The basic theme is one of gaining some degree of independence from a society fast approaching collapse. Independence may be agricultural (Tappan) or technological (Saxon); it may be expedient (Kearny) or planned well in advance (Clayton, Long, and McKeever). What these writers all share is a sense that "business as usual" must give way at least partially and temporarily to unusual preparations.

Another shared theme is a lack of confidence in the public sector. Cresson Kearny prefers civil defense to survivalism, yet he states that "I am not alone in concluding that the best short-term hope for improving Americans' chances of surviving a nuclear attack is for private organizations to make widely available field-tested, do-it-yourself survival instructions...and for concerned citizens to use these instructions to the best of their abilities." T.F. Nieman, an expert on fallout shelters, agrees: "each individual must be responsible for his own survival." Kurt Saxon's trust in subsistence farming and 19th century technology prompts him to state that "you can utilize the best of your ancestor's (sic) knowledge to ride out the worst of the chaos which is sure to come."

In the meantime, these survivalists' actions speak even louder than their words. Saxon lives in northern Arkansas; Clayton, in the California mountains; Kearny, in western Colorado; Duncan Long, in Kansas; Jim McKeever and Nancy Tappan, in southwestern Oregon.

To summarize these survivalist theoreticians' basic assumptions:
1. a catastrophe will happen soon;
2. nuclear war is the most likely;
3. anyone who wants to survive should get ready;
4. nobody should count on the government for help — or even *want* its help;
5. you're better off on your own.

The appearance of common ground is, however, somewhat deceptive. It is there, to be sure, but everything else which survivalists advocate can take vastly differing shapes. Survivalism may not be a movement — at least not in any organized sense — so much as a grassroots social trend. The "leaders" exemplify the trend as well as promote it. Their varied backgrounds and goals create some alliances, but also differences of opinion and even conflicts which override any sense of the shared purpose.

Many survivalists respect each other; some even work together. This is true of theoreticians as well as of rank and file survivalists. The writers who collaborate on *Personal Survival Letter*, for instance, know each other and share a general outlook on the movement (at least according to Bruce Clayton). Similarly, contributors and editors of *Survive* magazine — the first nationwide survivalist publication — seem more in tune than at odds with each other. There is, in addition, a kind of informal network of contacts among people who share beliefs and tactics. Intersections among local writers and theorists may increase now that Clayton has established his *Survivalist Directory*. (*Survive* magazine describes this project as "rather like computer dating — your shelter or mine?").

Yet other survivalists critcize and revile each other, sometimes even in public. There is a notorious rivalry in progress between Howard Ruff and Bob White, both hard-money survivalists. White has attacked Ruff for what he considers a less than 12% accuracy rate in his financial predictions; Ruff accuses White of "running a beautiful scam." Other survivalists fault each other for general incompetence. Many attack Ruff for his presumptuousness and haughtiness. One writer claims, "Ruff ignores everyone else in the movement. He doesn't allow me to sell my books at his conventions — it's as if he wants to keep his readers from knowing about other survivalists. The reason is that he doesn't really have the expertise to do what he's doing. His only real ability is self-promotion." When I asked how many other survivalists felt this way, the critic told me,

"Most of us don't feel very comfortable with Ruff." Another writer states that "Ruff has naive assumptions about the coming situation in the world."

One of the most frequently criticized survivvalists is Kurt Saxon. Saxon has a large following among southern and midwestern survivalists, and perhaps elsewhere as well; but his fellow-writers and newsletter-publishers hold him almost universally in contempt. Some of the reaction appears to be genuine revulsion toward his opinions. "The man is a flagrant racist," said one writer. Others fear that his opinions make all survivalists seem like crackpots. Some of the strongest attacks have nothing to do with Saxon's beliefs, but rather with his style. As another writer claims: "he's an exhibitionist."

Even more moderate survivalists draw criticism, though, simply for bringing the movement into the public arena. "Most survivalists are completely reticent," Bruce Clayton said; "they're not comfortable when someone gets a lot of attention." Ironically, survivalist theoreticians, by being prominent, automatically go against general sentiment by their willingness to face public scrutiny, but perhaps they regard this as a necessary evil. Some speak of their work with an almost missionary zeal. "The people *must* have this knowledge," T.F. Nieman maintains, while Howard Ruff (speaking of himself in the third person) says, "...anyone who knows Howard Ruff knows he is not just performing a service, he is on a crusade..." A Seattle survivalist described himself as "ready to wage total war against the enemies of the American people," while some of the moderates, though less shrill, are just as earnest. Cresson Kearny says, "My objective is to try to disseminate factual information so that something can be done to reduce the chances of nuclear war." But one consequence of so much publicity is that prominent survivalists often resent each other; and at times, even members of the rank and file criticize them, too, for drawing too much public attention.

Another factor is personality. Some of the theoreticians, regardless of their beliefs, simply don't get along. This may be a side-effect of tendencies toward introversion among survivalists. Mary McCarthy once said that two poets brooding on a beach are one poet too many, and perhaps something similar holds true for survivalists hiding out in the woods.

To what extent are the survivalist theoreticians really leaders? As with other aspects of the movement, this seems difficult to determine.

Most of the writers discussed here regard survivalism as their main occupation, but their activities and degrees of commitment may vary. At
least two have worked or still work with programs associated more
with civil defense than with survivalism: cresson Kearny worked for
the U.S. government civil defense programs in Tennessee, and more
recently has been "helping out" with an unspecified project in Utah;
in the meantime, Bruce Clayton has become civil defense director for
Mariposa County, California. For the others, including Long, Saxon,
and McKeever — leadership appears to be mostly a matter of running
the store. This is not to belittle their commitment to survivalist
theory; but regardless of their claims to spreading the word, most of
them   also stand to benefit materially as well as in other ways
from a favorable public response.

One possibility is that these leaders aren't leaders so much as
spokespersons. Instead of providing new perceptions, they simply
concentrate and articulate old ones. Some exceptions deserve special
note: cresson Kearny's development of certain expedient shelters, a
simple air pump, and do-it-yourself fallout meters are all genuine in-
novations; likewise, Mel Tappan's recommendations of specific
firearms appear to be a turning point — however dubious — in the
movement. But many other theoreticians have mostly just refor-
mulated data which others then acquire and reformulate yet again.
The issue at stake is not one of plagiarism or even originality. What
matters is whether the persons claiming to be authorities have
thought through the implications of what they advocate.

For instance, many survivalist writers gloss over gaps in their
own knowledge. More than one of them, while discussing complex
technical topics with potentially drastic consequences, will say, "The
dangers are hypothetical." It's hard to argue with them. Nobody has
much first-hand knowledge about the effects of nuclear weapons. But
the uncertainty hardly promises that the actual outcome will be
favorable. Writing of the ozone shield, for instance, Bruce Clayton in-
forms his readers that "Oxides of nitrogen in the quantities expected
from the detonation of 10,000 megatons will produce a significant
reduction in atmospheric ozone." And he goes on: "not much is yet
known about the UV threat (an increase in ultraviolet light as a consequence of ozone depletion) except that some plants seem to be very
sensitive to this type of light... That one is left hanging." Indeed it is.
And where does that leave us? Badly sunburned, it would appear. And
animals? Perhaps blinded by the millions. And plants? Nobody knows.

But the potential consequences on agriculture and even on the earth's oxygen supply are staggering. There's no point in denigrating Clayton's professional background; even a well-educated man, however, can suffer a dangerous failure of imagination.

The risk — here and elsewhere — is that the survivalist theoreticians appear not to be thinking through all of the consequences when they make claims and recommend courses of action. It's not simply that Kurt Saxon believes that a nuclear holocaust will be a blessing. Even the more astute survivalist writers seem not to perceive the side-effects of some of their theories and practices. Would the threat of nuclear war (as Cresson Kearny claims) "be decreased if any enemy nation knew that we had significantly improved our defenses?" Would it really (as Bruce Clayton asserts) "not be difficult to survive" a nuclear war? Perhaps these statements are correct. But they may be wrong instead. Even ascribing good intentions to the men who make them does not eliminate the possibility of bad insight. These survivalist theoreticians advocate courses of action which may produce entirely different results from what they expect.

Yet survivalist writers continue to dispense their opinions to worried individuals almost casually. Perhaps these writers are inadvertently telling people (and themselves) what they want to hear. If this is so, then the risk becomes a peculiar form of irresponsibility. It is a risk of mutual delusion. Again, these words aren't written to dismiss these theoreticians out of hand; since some of them make valid points. But many risk becoming not so much leaders as prominent followers. At some point, the survivalist theoreticians risk having to say what Gandhi once said under dramatically different circumstances, and with totally different effects: "there go my people. I must catch up with them, for I am their leader."

Chapter Three

Food Storage:
"Life Insurance You Can Eat"

The American food industry, though unquestionably the most productive in the world, is vulnerable to disruption in many ways. Modern agriculture relies so heavily on machinery that even a relatively minor problem, such as a fuel shortage, can limit operations; and farming depends on chemical fertilizers and pesticides, too, which are generally petroleum derivatives. Food processing is also highly mechanized. Similarly, distribution of food through truck and rail networks continues only through a constant influx of gasoline and diesel fuel. The American cornucopia feeds this country and dozens of other nations as well, but there is a catch: the system is a house of cards. Even a protracted oil embargo would damage it. A nuclear war would devastate it on every level — production, processing, and distribution — and would leave almost all survivors without sufficient food.

It is no surprise that food is an important issue to survivalists — particularly those worried about nuclear war. Even a "limited" war would severely harm American capacity for food production, since most military command centers, air bases, and missile silos (presumably the primary targets) are in breadbasket states like Wyoming, Montana, the Dakotas, Iowa, Wisconsin, and Illinois. An all-out war would effect every other farming state in the country. In addition, damage to roads, railroads, and vehicles would limit distribution of any remaining supplies available. The consequent likelihood of malnutrition and famine among survivors has therefore prompted many people to store emergency food supplies.

Food storage is, in fact, virtually the lowest common denominator among survivalist activities. There are a few members of the survival movement who decline to store food, and they warrant special attention. Whether bracing themselves for economic collapse, natural disaster or nuclear war, survivalists usually acquire food supplies and store them. Many store large quantities: a year's supply per person is common. Others store smaller amounts but wish to build up these reserves. In the words of one commercial supplier — words repeated by many survivalists as a kind of motto — food storage is "insurance you can *eat*!"

What people acquire, and how much, differs according to individual beliefs and financial means. At one end of the spectrum are those who simply buy more groceries than usual — canned goods and frozen foods, perhaps — and then rotate the stock; at the other end are those who purchase large quantities of freeze-dried or dehydrated provisions. A variety of companies have formed to meet the increased demands for these products. Some are scrupulous and offer high-quality goods. Others sell unimpressive or even defective merchandise. Almost all of them advertise in ways which stress a "better safe than sorry" theme. One of the most popular brands, Mountain House, puts out a leaflet asking, "COULD YOU SURVIVE A FOOD SHORTAGE?"

> If food supplies were interrupted, grocery stores could be out of fresh milk in a day or two; out of eggs, meat and poultry in a week; fresh fruits and vegetables would be scarce. Your money in the bank couldn't put food on your table — not the kind of food you enjoy now.... Not the wholesome food you need to stay healthy.

Neo-Life Company of America, another major food storage firm, advertises with a slick folder entitled, "Food for the Future." One section states, "It is hard to grasp the possibility of not having access to food, but common sense tells us it could happen. Common sense also tells us to protect ourselves and our family from major disasters by providing for them *ahead* of time." Many survivalists — including those who anticipate a nuclear war — respond strongly to these messages. Long-term food storage is now more common than at any time in decades.

For many years, the most organized and consistent practitioners of systematic food storage have been the Mormons. The Mormon intentions aren't specifically geared toward a war — nuclear or otherwise; rather, there is a general emphasis on emergency preparedness within this church. One Mormon writer, Brian Kelly, states in *Survive* magazine that:

> accident, illness, unemployment or various shortages can affect any household at almost any time. In addition, there are other possibilities to prepare for that are less likely, but could happen just the same. Wars, depressions, famines, earthquakes, floods and tornados should be kept in mind when planning a storage system.

Although worries about nuclear war make up only part of this agenda, the Mormon influence on more self-consciously survivalist groups makes it important to examine closely what the Mormons do in storing food.

Mormon food storage is not a new phenomenon; on the contrary, it is a long-standing custom. Perhaps it originates in the group's experience of settling a harsh and sparsely populated terrain. More recent events, however, have intensified concerns about food within the Church of Jesus Christ of Latter-Day Saints. During the Great Depression, LDS leaders established a policy which made individual members responsible to concentric circles of their community: first their own family, then their local church community, then the community at large. Responsibilities include the storage of food as a hedge against hard times. A 1977 speech by Spencer W. Kimball, President of the Church, encouraged families to set goals of preparedness in physical, social, emotional and spiritual terms. The result has been extensive food storage. Many Mormon families store at least one year's worth of food for its members. Standard supplies include wheat, powdered milk, honey or sugar, and salt. In addition, some Mormon communities maintain grain silos and other facilities for the purpose of storing emergency supplies.

The Denver stake (regional group of LDS churches) is characteristic of how the Mormons promulgate policy on food storage. Church leaders in Salt Lake City appoint a member to coordinate activities in an area and this person them takes on specific duties that include recommendations to the individual wards (churches), providing information about where to obtain food, and — if necessary — distributing communal supplies in the event of a disaster. In Denver, this coordinator also oversees the operations of an LDS-owned grain silo and cannery.

"There's no *policy* as such," says Harry Bullock, the current food storage coordinator in the Denver stake; "there are *plans*. Families' needs differ. We have various suggestions which people can implement — lists of what they need. We don't require anything." However, individual members of the LDS church have told me that recommendations are serious; and although there is not strict enforcement of them, Mormons exert at least subtle pressure on each other through social expectation. Most families comply at least to some degree. According to Merle Allen, a Mormon merchant in Denver, some fifty percent of local LDS families store food for long-term use, while others own more limited stocks. The communal silo reputedly contains enough wheat to feed this large Mormon community for two or three months.

The purpose of LDS policy — and apparently its successful result — is to prepare each Mormon family to meet its concentric circles of responsibility. This is not necessarily a survivalist agenda; it responds to personal as well as societal emergencies, minor as well as major. Merle Allen explains, "The LDS attitude is simply cautious. It recognizes that life is unpredictable. You don't have to have a huge calamity hit you. A man could simply lose his job — then what would his family eat?" However, Mormon attitudes often overlap with survivalist concerns. The relatively greater number of Mormons in the western United States, including desolate areas of Utah, Colorado, and Nevada, make these people sensitive to the uncertainties of weather and their geographical isolation. Fears of social collapse or nuclear war heighten a sense of vulnerability, and yet the impulse to store food has already been there a long time.

What are the more specifically survivalist plans for food storage? Many of them are "high tech" extensions of Mormon attitude. Bruce Clayton, for instance, writing in *Life After Doomsday*, outlines four basic approaches to "constructing an emergency food stockpile." They are:

1. canned, boxed, and otherwise processed supermarket foods, rotated periodically to maintain freshness;
2. the Mormon "basic four" approach — bulk containers of wheat, sugar or honey, powdered milk, and salt;

3. commercially packed air dried or freeze dried foods;
4. nutritional supplements — vitamins and protein powders.

Clayton suggests a combination of these approaches because the canned, air dried, and freeze dried foods provide variety; the "basic four" foods provide cheap supplies in greater abundance; and the supplements fill in the gaps. In addition, Clayton recommends acquiring equipment for gardening and food preservation.

Cresson Kearny also advocates storing a variety of foods, but his emphases resemble those of the Mormon approach more consistently than do Clayton's. *Nuclear War Survival Skills* includes information on what to store — grain, beans, vegetable oil, sugar, salt, and vitamin pills — and how to process these foods into a relatively varied diet. Kearny also advocates storing special foods for children and the elderly.

Other survivalist writers and theoreticians vary these food storage programs according to individual preferences and biases. Mel Tappan, for example, stresses a plan almost identical to Clayton's, the chief exception being a preference for dehydrated over freeze dried foods. Duncan Long remains vague about specifics ("You need to be all but self-sufficient") but seems to urge storage of long-term food supplies and implements for subsistence farming. Distributors and "survival consultants" tend, of course, to recommend that survivalists buy their own line of goods; and some of these consultants — Howard Ruff, for instance — have inspired criticism even from fellow survivalists for possible conflict-of-interest.

In the meantime, it is worth noting that some factions within the survival movement overlap considerably with the "back-to-the-land" movement. Ten years ago, they would not have been called survivalists at all, but rather communards. Many organic gardeners and advocates of "soft" technology (windmills, biomass, solar energy) in turn strive for a level of independence or even isolation from the wider society which makes them almost indistinguishable from certain kinds of survivalists. This seems particularly true in regard to food storage. Survivalists and back-to-the-landers share a concern for the vulnerability of American food production and distribution systems, and they strive for a similar kind of independence even though their styles and rhetoric differ. Nancy Tappan, for instance, whose chief interest is self-sufficient farming, states, "What I'm doing with my life is no different than what the majority of people in this country did until a generation or two ago. I take delight in getting back to the basic rhythms of life." Meanwhile, back-to-the-land magazines like *Mother Earth News* provide information which many survivalists adapt to their own programs.

And what are the rank and file survivalists doing about food? As usual, Bruce Clayton *Survivalist Directory* gives some interesting indications. Clayton's analyzes the responses of the 161 survivalists listed by stating that:

> Most people have already stocked between six and eighteen months of supplies. Some have five year's (sic) worth. Some are supplied for as little as one week.   These last are not as well prepared as they would like.... Nearly everyone seemed to be still adding to the stockpile as finances allowed.

The most consistent activity seems to be storage of dehydrated or freeze dried supplies. For example, AR4 writes that he has "At least a year's supply of soybeans, corn, wheat, rye, lentils, rice, nutritional yeast, alfalfa seeds and several cases of Pro-Vita dehydrated foods." WI1 maintains "a six month supply of all types of food on a rotational basis. CO3 has acquired "very substantial amounts of food: bulk grains and beans, canned goods, dried eggs, powdered milk, juices, 'and all other types of foods to give a balanced diet.' " TN3 describes storing "a year's worth of food, mostly grain." These comments are characteristic of most entries in the *Directory*.

In addition, however, many survivalists listed there plan to raise some or all of their food on farms or ranches. Some of them have already achieved a remarkable degree of self-sufficiency. FL3 has a self-sufficient rural retreat, since he "grew up on a farm (and) has the skills to operate it." Similarly, OK1 states that "with present supplies, paid-for retreat, hunting, fishing, gardening,...unlimited timber and water, I could exist comfortably indefinitely..." Others have not yet acquired this degree of independence, but are striving for it. WI2 explains that:

> We have been living on a small farmette and have been exploring various areas of self-sufficiency for several years. We hope to be vegetable and grain independent with limited livestock (bees, chickens, goats and probably pork). Probable labor/food cooperation with local rancher and farmers. Except to supplement with big and small game trapping and especially fishing.

TX4. meanwhile, "wants to be close to the food supply," and, if given ten acres, "could produce a surplus of food" by employing previous skills. Others, like FL7, plan "to grow, raise, trap, hunt and gather what we need."

A related issue to personal food storage is whether survivalists are willing to feed non-survivalists in the event of an emergency. Clayton asked applicants to the *Directory*, "Have you laid aside any extra food to feed your unprepared neighbors or relatives?" Most people answered "no" or left the question blank; others, however, stated that they had either stored some food for this purpose or hoped to do so. VA1, for instance, feels that "extra food for unprepared relatives and at least a few refugees/neighbors should be part of a complete stockpile." KS1 has stocked "a large supply of Civil Defense surplus crackers for animal feed and emergency food..." which he might share with neighbors or relatives. CA2 "has no food stored for unprepared relatives," but he states that "I like the idea." Other survivalists would be willing to share supplies under certain conditions. "We would have to share with other believers as commanded by God," said MO1, while CA32 claims that he would be willing "to feed several others, if they are ready to work and ready to eat what I offer (plenty but monotonous)." These responses dispute the stereotype of survivalists as invariably hoarding food and intent only on serving their own purpose. In fact, several listings in the *Directory* suggest a kind of social conscience within the movement. Clayton writes of CA1 that:

> When he first moved into the mountaintop community, he took with him a two-year supply of everything he would ever need, not just food... However he noticed that no one else in the community was "prepared" in any significant way. It seemed obvious that in a prolonged disaster he would either have to share his food with 126 neighboring families...and quickly join them in starvation...or he would have to turn them away empty-handed and risk eventual violence...
> He didn't like either alternative, so he created a third choice ...surround himself with dozens of families also prepared for any disaster. He spent hundreds of hours writing a local survivalist newsletter, holding monthly meetings in his home, teaching classes, buying supplies in bulk (last trip was for another 15,000 pounds of wheat), and in general pushing, prodding, and pulling his neighboring families into buying a year's supply of food, he also talked them into buying another year's worth for the remaining neighbors!

However, some survivalists are unquestionably possesive of their supplies — even violently so. FL3 speaks of a willingness to "defend (his) retreat to the death." SD2 states that, "No, I do not stock food, water or supplies for anyone other than my wife. What I do is stock explosive trip devices at my doors, weapons and munitions for any un-invited guests." And TX5, who owns a 10-acre tract, explains what many of his fellow survivalists seem to feel:

> It is my belief that food is going to be the key to survival in the days ahead.... Consider the fact that over 95% of the food in this country is produced by less than 10% of the people. A lot of people must buy their daily bread. Should those who produce the food one day refuse to trade an item of definite value for a piece of colored paper...(?)

My own correspondence with survivalists reflects a similar variety and intensity of feelings about food. Almost all survivalists store food; how they do it, though, and with what intentions, ranges greatly. Since most of them sacrifice something — time, money, ef-fort, or all three — to make their survival preparations, these people resent their friends' and relatives' skepticism or mockery. It is the classic Grasshopper vs. Ant dilemma. And the resentment seems to overwhelm most survivalists' potential for good intentions.

Clayton summed up the issue this way:

> Several (survivalists) said that they had in fact laid in extra food for relatives...several tons of it in one case. Many people com-mented that this would be a good idea but they wanted to finish their own emergency stockpile first. There were also several strikingly negative responses, however. The basic theme was that people who don't prepare deserve to starve. Some of this seemed due to an endorsement of natural selection, while other entries showed clear personal resentment against close family members who would not assist in preparing the retreat, but who joked in bad taste about showing up to be fed anyway if things did go wrong.

As for the food itself — dozens of companies offer their customers a wide range of products. The three biggest producers of survival food — Mountain House, Neo-Life, and Sam Andy Foods — produce not only individual products, but also comprehensive storage plans. These range from Neo-Life's Porta Pack of sixty meals to huge assortments which could feed a family for years. Most of the foods are either dehydrated or freeze dried. The larger companies provide detailed nutritional information and generally make a good case for the variety and quality of their products. These include fruits, vegetables, meats, and TVP's (textured vegetable proteins), eggs and dairy products, legumes and grains, salads, snacks, crackers, beverages, and desserts. (Mountain House even puts out freeze-dried ice cream in three flavors: chocolate, strawberry, and vanilla.)

Anyone who has ever eaten backpacking provisions would know what this food is like, since the long-term food storage companies are often the same ones that produce camping supplies. It is not exactly *haute cuisine.* (Some enterprising soul is surely going to start a line of emergency foods for the gourmet, however: perhaps freeze-dried *Coquilles Saint-Jacques Sautees a la Provencale* and dehydrated Pouille-Fuisse? For health-food nuts, there is already Simpler Life Food Storage — "No Chemicals! Organically Grown!") Most current products have either a salty, TV dinner-ish tang or else a blandness which makes everything seem boiled. It's not the sort of food that many people would crave under most circumstances. Perhaps the key word is still "emergency." Even the pickiest connoisseur would devour a bowlful of Neo-Life's Country Stew for lack of any alternative. As Cervantes said, "There's no sauce in the world like hunger."

I spent most of a week eating survival food as an experiment, and emerged from my kitchen-lab somewhat bloated but otherwise none the worse off. This food isn't actually much different from a lot of ordinary American supermarket and restaurant fare; the producers of emergency food have gone out of their way to simulate real meat-'n'-potatoes cooking. In my case, the test-run evoked many memories of camping expeditions, which perhaps altered my perceptions somewhat. These products are also amusing to prepare. It's strange to watch what resembles nothing so much as straw puff up into Tuna a la Neptune. Stranger still, a piece of pink styrofoam transforms itself into rib-eye steak. Ugly yellow powder turns into butter. A colorless sponge turns into — of all things — vanilla ice cream. Some of the appeal of survival food is knowing that a compact stack of boxes can yield a nearly unending cornucopia.

Food storage is probably the most benign of survivalist activities, yet the phenomenon brings up some tricky ethical questions. The one

asked most often concerns hoarding. Is it right to accumulate big supplies of food in a world where one third of the population is
malnourished? Survivalists and others reply that the food they *don't*
buy won't miraculously appear in the slums of Lima, Calcutta, or
Chicago. Some even argue that their own private stashes may work to
the common good, at least in the long run: they will never need to rely
on public sources in times of scarcity. Such arguments are difficult to
refute. There is certainly no magic way of teleporting food from one
place to another, and Mormon self-reliance during the Great Depression gives credence to the second claim. However, the arguments are
simplistic in not acknowledging the basic problems of distribution not
only in the Third World, but throughout the United States as well.
Here as in other ways, "Them that has, gits."

Where survivalists make a better case for their activities is in
claiming historical precedent. The fact of the matter is that long-term
food storage is an old idea, not a new one, and is still practiced
throughout much of the world. For millenia, most inhabitants of the
planet have survived only by careful acquiring, storing, and rationing
of supplies. What is new is the American 7-11 mentality — dropping
by the store on a moment's notice. But since the systems that supply
our supermarkets — farming, harvesting, shipping, processing, more
shipping, marketing, and still more shipping — require huge outputs
of labor and energy, it's no surprise that the whole business should
start to seem fragile and inefficient. It *is* fragile and inefficient. Crop
damage (such as drought in the Midwest or Medflies in California)
could limit availability of many goods. Another oil embargo could
paralyze distribution. People who store food aren't necessarily
paranoid.

Still, the basic issue remains: is long-term food storage any
solution? Immediately we have to ask, "Solution to *what?*" If the
problem is personal misfortune — injury or loss of a job — then
perhaps owning some dehydrated or freeze-dried food could soften the
blow. If the problem is a local disaster — an earthquake, a blizzard, or
a flood — then even a modest stash of supplies could make a big difference to oneself, one's family, and one's neighbors. However, if the
problem is a massive, long-term disaster — especially a nuclear war,
then food may not be the hedge it seems.

The food storage companies want us to believe that we're "better
safe than sorry." It's hard to argue against such an age-old motto. Yet
in the aftermath of a nuclear attack (and surely this is what most sur-

vivalists consider the object of their preparations) how much safety would even ten years' worth of food provide?

We should explore two other aspects of the survivalist agenda before answering this question.

Chapter Four

Shelter

"If livin' was a thing that money could buy..."

This advertisement appeared in a major American newspaper:

ARE YOUR LOVED ONES PROTECTED?

Have You Prepared for Survival?

Don't wait - - - NOW is the time!
Fallout Shelters/Concussion Chambers

NO MONEY DOWN

Open 24 hours a day

A sign of the times: typical Eighties survivalism. Right?
Wrong. The ad — and dozens like it — showed up in 1961. And although the Sixties "shelter scare," as some people called it, was the most intense outburst of nuclear worries up to that time, even so it wasn't the first. The fact remains that Americans started debating the issues of shelter almost as soon as the fallout cooled off at Hiroshima and Nagasaki.

The debate heated up once the Soviet Union detonated its first atomic bomb in 1949, and part of the debate concerned whether the shelters in question should be public or private. *Time* magazine, for instance, reported in its December 18, 1950 issue that "The Federal Civil Defense Administration...announced last week that it planned to provide bomb shelters for 50 million people in critical target areas."

Some citizens received the news skeptically. Mrs. Alf Heiberg of
Washington D.C., was one who responded by arranging to build her
own shelter — in this case, something large enough to accomodate
100 to 150 of her neighbors. "I wouldn't enjoy sealing myself up if I
knew my neighbors were being blown to bits," she explained. By the
winter of 1951, as *Time* stated in a February 5 article, "dozens of new
construction firms appeared, offering everything from $13.50 foxhole
shelters to luxurious $5.500 suites equipped with telephone, escape
hatches, bunks, toilets and Geiger counter."

Then, during the late Fifties and early Sixties, interest in fall-out
shelters reached a kind of critical mass. The previously random newspaper and magazine articles now turned into a chain reaction. *Time*,
Saturday Evening Post, *Life*, and other popular magazines quickly
reported the trend in stories entitled, "Bomb Shelter Build Up," "Cof-
fins or Shields?" and "Everybody's Talking about Shelters." Other
publications, some of scholarly or religious bent, questioned the
wisdom of what they regarded as a dangerous fad. *The Christian Century* published an article called "Morality Requires Community
Shelters." A writer in *The New Republic* wondered "Who Shall Be
Saved by Shelters?" Even *Good Housekeeping* leaped into the fray:
"Let's Stop the Fall-out Shelter Folly!"

The debate wasn't simply journalistic. As *Life* reported in October of 1961:

> All of a sudden everybody is talking about it — at PTA
> meetings, at bridge parties, on intercontinental airliners and on
> suburban trains, over the back fence and — since women no
> longer meet at the well — at supermarkets....
>   Almost overnight the realization has grown among millions
> of Americans that they must face this problem — one which
> many others still shun as "too terrible to contemplate."

The editors of *Life* went on to state that "This growing interest and action has now translated itself into the nation's official goal," and that
with the goal being set, "there can be no doubt that it will be met as
America has met past emergencies with speed, know-how, and calm efficiency."

But by the mid-Sixties, the fallout shelter boom had diminished
and faded. A quick glance at any year-by-year summary of related articles is astonishing: what had been dozens, even hundreds during 1961
drops to five or ten during 1964. "Do We Want Shelters?" asked *The*

Bulletin of the Atomic Scientists, while *Newsweek* reports: "No Market for Shelters." During the late Sixties, it was rare to find any news about fallout shelters at all. So much for speed, know-how, and calm efficiency.

What happened? The question would take a sociologist to answer, but one possibility is that the Cuban Missile Crisis of October, 1962, shook up Americans in a way that made further interest in shelters impossible to sustain. Perhaps the near-miss scared most people enough that they refused to contemplate nuclear disaster at all. Perhaps the relative lack of conflict during the years preceding American involvement in Vietnam lulled people out of their previous panic. Whatever caused it, however, the change itself is undeniable.

There is now a revival of interest in fallout and even blast shelters throughout the United States. Not all of the interest orginates within the survivalist movement; some advocates of shelter construction are, in fact, convinced that programs must be public, not private, and hence are in some senses anti-survivalist. (A later chapter examines the similarities and differences between survivalism and civil defense.) On the other hand, many survivalists regard civil defense as important, too — if only because public programs would take the pressure off them in the event of an actual war. The point for the moment is simply that the debate is again underway.

It is more than a debate. Nationwide, there is now more construction of shelters than at any time since the early Sixties. Much of this activity reflects the common survivalist concern that the United States lacks a workable program to defend its citizens from the effects of nuclear war. As with other survivalist concerns, the problem is not imaginary, though some of the actions it produces are questionable. Bardyl Tirana, the U.S. Director of Civil Defense in 1978, even expressed his own misgivings: "We have no civil defense program, merely the apparatus to start one." The response of many survivalists — as in other situations — has been to take the matter into their own hands.

Among the survivalist theoreticians, some are prominent specifically for advocating private shelters. Thomas F. Nieman is one of them. His book, *Better "Read" Than Dead: The Complete Book of Nuclear Survival*, aims to "present as accurately as possible...the comprehensive plans and strategy available for nuclear survival planning." It is essentially a compendium of materials available elsewhere.

However, Nieman frames his information with the argument that current civil defense preparations in the United States are not just inadequate, but dangerous, and that only private initiative can rescue the American people from catastrophe.

> The government claims it cannot afford to allocate massive funds into the American civil defense system, let alone support a city or countrywide shelter policy. However, the U.S. cannot afford **not** to have a comprehensive civil defense program. There is no doubt that at the present time this country is in serious economic trouble, yet the individual can keep the candle of hope alive.

Nieman stresses that **"THE FREE ENTERPRISE SYSTEM OF THE UNITED STATES CAN RESCUE THIS NATION."**

Nieman claims to explain how. After a brief overview of nuclear weapons (history, categories, effects, misconceptions), he specifies what he considers the alternatives for survival. He believes that publicly financed civil defense is out of the question because of bureaucratic ineptitude, wishful thinking, and outright foolishness; the nuclear strategy called Mutually Assured Destruction and the civil defense plan called Crisis Relocation incur his greatest wrath. Consequently, Nieman devotes the rest of the book to the details of individual survival. *Better "Read" Than Dead* contains maps of high-risk areas, information on how to interpret them, data on calculating radiation doses, and various plans for constructing blast and fallout shelters. (Most of these plans are standard U.S. Department of Defense information.) In conclusion, Nieman reiterates his belief that:

> If a war were to occur now, the only help that you as an individual are likely to get is the help you can provide yourself through prior planning. If you are interested in insuring (sic) your own survival, and the survival of your family, it is imperative that you take the steps outlined in this book.

Other theoreticians are more influential than Nieman, though they share some or all of his convictions. Cresson Kearny, for instance, also holds U.S. Government civil defense plans in contempt, and advocates individual action instead; unlike Nieman, he provides detailed instructions based on his own reasearch at the Oak Ridge National Laboratory in Tennessee. These instructions not only deal with technical background for surviving a nuclear attack, but also many aspects of preparation. He explains that:

> If average Americans are to do their best when building expedient shelters and life-support equipment for themselves, they need detailed information... We are not a people accustomed to blindly following orders. Unfortunately, during a crisis threatening nuclear war, it would take too long to read instructions explaining why each important feature was designed as specified.

Kearny's reputation as a kind of elder statesman within the survival movement, however, inclines most survivalists to trust his recommendations. These include acquiring skills in advance, learning to build auxiliary equipment like the Kearny Air Pump, and building expedient shelters during the emergency itself. "By following the instructions in this book," Kearny says about *Nuclear War Survival Skills*, "you and your family can increase the odds favoring your survival."

Some people don't especially want to acquire these skills, yet wish to take precautions against nuclear war anyway. One result of this ambivalence is a growing business of fallout shelter construction.

Among these are general contractors and other companies which build shelters as a sideline. Arcwright and Hutcher Construction, for instance, is a Denver firm which undertakes such projects at the customers' request. Speaking about company policy, Don Griffiths, an Arcwright and Hutcher engineer, explains that "Our standard *modus operandi* is to refer customers to the standard Civil Defense literature. We urge them to do their shelter themselves." If a customer insists, then Arcwright and Hutcher will go ahead. "Sometimes this is beefing up part of a basement," according to Griffiths. "Or if we're doing a commercial installation, sometimes the customer wants a shelter, and so we make provisions." Nonetheless it appears that this sort of company finds shelter construction less than compelling work. Griffiths adds, "We could get a lot of business on this exploiting the trend, but it isn't our kind of sales."

Other companies are not so reluctant. There is, in fact, what appears to be a booming business in fallout and even blast shelters. As during the 1950s, some of these firms spring up overnight, and the quality of their products may be questionable. A growing number of firms seem to be striving for reliable service, however. Some see themselves as carrying out an important mission. One of them, Nuclear Fallout Shelter and Bombshelter Supply and Construction Company, located in Muncy Valley, Pennsylvania, builds both private and industrial shelters. Calvin Zehring, the president of this company, boasts that it is one of only "two firms in the United States and the United Kingdom which offers the full spectrum of shelters and supplies which are necessary for survival..."

Despite this claim, however, other companies are now successfully marketing various kinds of shelters. Biosphere Corporation of Greenfield, New Hampshire, is one of them. This firm specializes in designing, building, and installing 8 by 15 foot egg-shaped shelters throughout the United States. *The Egg* — as John Brodie, its inventor, calls it — includes ventilation, water storage, waste disposal, and other environmental systems. In addition, the Biosphere Corporation decorates the Eggs with bright colors to "erase the confining aspects of a small space." Brodie states that "greater attention should be focused on the psychological aspects of shelter living," and therefore his company attempts to provide more than a mere refuge. The price: $14,000 plus delivery and installation charges for a basic Egg.

Other suppliers of shelters and shelter plans are Stormaster Shelter Company of Dallas, Texas; and Underground Homes of Portsmouth, Ohio. Stormaster Shelter Company builds elliptical concrete blast shelters "capable of withstanding a 10-megaton blast only one kilometer distant," according to *Survive* magazine (July/August, 1982). Available only in Texas, this shelter costs $5-10,000. In contrast, the plans available through Underground Homes are not intended simply for an emergency shelter, but rather for a subterranean house of conventional size. Such houses have drawn attention primarily for their energy efficiency; interest in their protection from fallout is a recent phenomenon. They are popular among many people who prefer not to see themselves as head-for-the-hills survivalists.

Alternatively, some people want to accomodate a degree of nuclear protection into new or existing homes, but use more traditional sources of help in their efforts. Some seek out architects to design their fallout shelters. One such architect is Richard L. Crowther, a specialist in solar homes, who practices in Denver. During the early 1960s, Crowther became a fallout shelter analyst (certified by the Office of Civil Defense Mobilization) because of his "concern about fallout from an accident or a war." Crowther built a small shelter in his own house in 1961, and designed shelters for some of his clients as well.

Since then, however, he has come to question the value of shelters — at least in a high-risk area like Denver — because of nuclear proliferation. "It wouldn't be worth it now," he told me. "It had more credibility in the Sixties. I'm basically skeptical about people's chances of surviving a war, though it (a shelter) makes more sense if there's an accident." Crowther is nonetheless willing to incorporate shelters into his clients' homes if they so request. "I'm doing a house with a shelter right now," he says. What is his procedure for dealing with people who want this service? "I try to tell them about the reality of the situation. It's not blast protection, and it may not be adequate fallout protection for the area. If we had a nuclear attack, Denver would be heavily irradiated. Rocky Flats (a nuclear weapons facility) is one of the primary targets." Do people have realistic expectations about shelters and whatever measure of security they provide? "Most people don't really know. I think the problem they overlook is the problem involved in long-term habitation."

Regardless, many survivalists have made 1950s style preparations — (basement and backyard shelters) while others would like to build something along these lines. Of those listed in Bruce Clayton's *Survivalist Directory*, for instance, eighteen respondents state that they own a completed or nearly completed shelter. MA3 mentions having "a fall-out shelter under construction," and gives the reason for lack of faster progress: "Money — lack thereof." TX2, NY2, KS1, and NM1 each mention small but finished shelters. Others describe more elaborate preparations. MT1 states that he is "building one in my basement right now but will be leaving it behind shortly," and adds that "I hope to build at next move from ground up, incorporating shelter right into house as rec room or root cellar." The largest system listed in the *Directory* appears to be CA37's: his property contains two fallout shelters, "a cave which would hold 20-30 people, and a mine, wet in winter, which if set up would hold 50 people."

Some survivalists have made unusual — even outlandish — claims about their preparations, and assessing them is often difficult. One of the most ambitious (or fanciful) survivalists wrote to me late in 1981 and stated that his house is a "virtual atomic war survival center for up to 50 people..."

> It is so fool proof (sic) that any passer by (sic) on the street sees a crummy ordinary (sic) front, sides, and back walls. Inside I have several rooms, bolted if need be, for survival. I can last 10 years inside never going out... I spent 5 months in it. Not coming out once. None of my friends could break in.

Others have indicated more conventional efforts. A young man who lives in a Long Island town explained that so far, he has built an underground backyard fallout/blast shelter, a greenhouse, and a camper survival vehicle, but that he also regards these as only an initial phase of reaching long-term goals. These include "domestic and foreign retreat; mobility (land, sea, air); and earth-sheltered homesteads at both domestic and foreign sites." Of his primary site shelter, he says:

> It is constructed of corrugated steel pipe 6' in diameter. The overall length is 34'. Outfitted to sleep 8 persons! It has a protection factor of at least 1/1000 since it is buried with 6 feet of earth covering. A radiological filter is situated several feet away and scrubs particles drawn into the shelter through a blower system. A dub well will pump ground water into the shelter using a hand pump. I am outfitting the shelter for chemical and biological warfare protection and am including a supply of oxygen for fire storm protection.

Another man, R.V., a 41-year-old survivalist in downstate New York, believes that his preparations make him "ready for any emergency. We live in an area which is far enough from any primary targets as to afford fairly good protection from thermal blast. Our only problem would be that of fallout. Although I do not have a fallout shelter per se, it would not take long to make our basement perfectly safe."

Most survivalists who currently lack a shelter seem to regret it. Thirteen say so outright in Clayton's *Directory*; others seem to imply it by talking around the issue. TX8 states that his "worst problem" is not having "the real estate layout needed to construct an adequate fallout shelter." Similarly, AL1 speaks of planning "to start building an underground house" after finishing school. NY3 laments not having a fallout shelter because he rents a house, and NC4 worries because "my home is not situated in a very defendable area and the water table is high, which complicates the construction of an adequate concealed fallout/blast shelter." WI1, meanwhile, plans "a fallout shelter with shielding factor of 1500 that will house ten people easily." Of those who would like a shelter but cannot afford it, NC4 puts the situation most bluntly: "We do not have a real fallout shelter yet and it is driving us crazy."

In addition to traditional shelters, some novel alternatives exist. One is the "survival home." Survival homes are those designed and constructed with specific and sometimes comprehensive survival measures in mind. All houses, of course, imply concern for survival, since human beings almost always require protection from their environment; but proponents of survival homes advocate much more focused attention to external threats.

Joel Skousen is currently one of the leading advocates of this concept. His company, Survival Homes Corporation, based in Hood River, Oregon, is an architectural firm which specializes in "maximum security homes" and "self-sufficient homes." When I spoke with Skousen about his firm, he told me, "We cover the entire gamut of situations. Not everyone needs the same thing. A lot of general (survivalist) recommendations can have consequences ranging from benign to disastrous." Survival Homes Corporation therefore provides more specific advice on how clients should prepare themselves. Some of this advice goes against popular wisdom. "Some of the common generalizations — such as leaving town for the country — can be dangerous. Cutting your financial lifeline would kill you faster than mobs of people. We work with a client and assess their desires, concerns, and financial picture. Maybe they should stay in the suburbs instead of going to rural areas. Then we design the home for specific threats."

Depending on his assessment, Skousen and his associates recommend particular options. These vary according to whether the client fears financial collapse, urban unrest, ordinary crime, nuclear war, or other dangers. All, however, stress some sort of interior stronghold. The stronghold is not only a fallout shelter, but is a self-contained survival center, often complete with electrical generators, water supply, and other life support systems. It is also undetectable. This secretive facet of Skousen's designs is what sets them apart from many other kinds of survivalist shelter. A survival home of this sort is relatively safe not because it looks like a fortress, but rather because it doesn't. Skousen stresses inconspicuousness. He also downplays the common emphasis on weapons. He told me, "We believe that owners are going to need arms, but we don't believe in relying on weapons. They should be the last resort. Technology isn't going to help people. If you shoot off a lot of guns, someone's just going to come with something bigger. You should keep a low profile."

In short, Skousen advocates shelter which is more than shelter in the 1960s sense, but also less: the stronghold itself is sophisticated, yet outsiders would have a hard time even finding it. Clients who want this kind of system apparently regard the hold-the-fort survivalists in contempt. They would rather fade into the woodwork.

Skousen admits to some special problems with his recommendations: "The equipment is phenomenally expensive." Electrical systems for a survival home will cost about $25,000, and equipment in general will run $70-200,000 — "not counting the house." "There's been no noticeable increase in the number of people who can afford these homes," Skousen told me, "but there's been a massive, overwhelming interest from people in general — many who can't afford them. There's a lot of misinformation around. People don't realize that it's going to cost them $200,000 *minimum* for self-sufficiency. I'm not talking about the subsistence farming route. You can still do that. But if you want to maintain your current lifestyle, it's another matter." He went on to say that "People get angry at us — as if it's our fault. I wish we could do it differently, but these are the realities of technology."

Other survival planners attempt different solutions to technological problems. Lane Blackmore, president of Survive Tomorrow, Inc., has established what he calls the "ark" concept. This involves carefully engineered structures capable of housing dozens or even hundreds of people. They are not community projects; on the contrary, they are privately funded efforts well in keeping with the common survivalist bias toward free enterprise. When I spoke with Blackmore during summer of 1982, he told me about his current project, *Terrene Ark 1.* This complex — 240 "survival condominiums" in southwestern Utah — is well under way. Appoximately 25% of the units have already been sold. (Prices range from $26,000 for a studio apartment to $96,000 for a three-bedroom suite.) The Terrene Ark includes decontamination chambers, ventilation systems, 200,000 gallons of emergency water, electrical generators, heavy protection from fallout, and round-the-clock security. In addition, each unit comes complete with "four man-years of food at 2,400 calories and 85 grams of protein per day."

This project may well be technologically superior to individual attempts to obtain survival shelter, but is it in other ways? Blackmore claims that it is. First of all, he rejects the argument that the Terrene Ark is part of mainstream survivalism. "I used to see myself as a survivalist," he told me, "but then I realized that the principle of survival is really the community. If you stand back from the community, you see that you're abandoning the best part of life — people. The beauty of society is interdependence. And so I wanted to build something within the human community." Then why is he off in the Utah desert? Like many survivalists, Blackmore seems to see his course of action as making the best of dangerous times. "People are frustrated because they don't have a vehicle for expressing their fears of nuclear war. Look — we want the bomb put away, but the risks are still there. I don't see all-out anarchy coming; but I see a limited nuclear war. The Russians, with their knowledge of civil defense, will make an adversary we can't buffalo. Our own willingness to act on self-defeating principles is much of the problem." In response to these risks, he advocates doing "something which would give Americans some resiliency. The idea of having the Terrene Ark as an alternative to retreating is very precious to me."

As Ron Boutwell, the public relations director for Survive Tomorrow, Inc., explained recently, "The STI concept of survival advocates a group survival effort as opposed to an individual one. Only group survival allows for a pooling of resources and skills and a continuing cohesive society. Only group survival can provide the necessities of civilization." He may be right. Whether Terrene Ark I provides "the necessities of civilization" is another matter. In any case — and despite Blackmore's plans for building shelters of a cheaper, "more austere" sort — the fact remains that survival in La Verkin, Utah, requires at least $26,000.

Some survivalists own shelters; others buy condominiums. Still others, however, have gone a step further. They see a fallout or blast shelter as only one aspect of their preparations. The 1960s shelter advocates built shelters but otherwise changed few of their activities; in contrast, some contemporary survivalists make drastic changes in their lives. These are the "retreaters." (Many survivalists, including theoreticians like Bruce Clayton, use the words survivalist and retreater interchangeably, though "survivalist" has become more prevalent.) These survivalists have established or want to establish a retreat at a distance from their normal dwelling place; or else they have withdrawn entirely. They have literally headed for the hills.

Two of the survivalist theoreticians who have been most influential in this regard are Mel Tappan and Nancy Tappan. Writing in the first issue of *Personal Survival Letter*, Mel Tappan states that "no

program of long-term survival preparedness is viable" which fails to
provide adequately for (among other things) "a safe place sensibly
remote from areas of high population density." His book *Tappan on
Survival* elaborates on this assumption.

> The concept most fundamental to realistic long-term dis-
> aster preparedness is retreating; having a safe place to go in
> order to avoid the concentrated violence destined to erupt in the
> cities — a place where, in addition to owning greater safety dur-
> ing the crisis interval, one can reasonably expect to generate
> subsistence for an indefinite period thereafter.

(Tappan regarded this agenda as even more important in the
event of a nuclear disaster.) He adds that "Despite its central importance to the business of staying alive...this aspect of the survival equa-
tion is not widely understood." The reason, according to Tappan, is
that too many people think of retreating in hackneyed terms; survival
literature often "seems to confuse the romance of woodcraft,
nomadics and homesteading with the hard realities of disaster survival."

Tappan's agenda is therefore to examine the inadequate or even
dangerous options (such as "the sea-going approach," "the land
mobile techniques," "isolated wilderness retreats," and "group
retreats") and then to advocate what he considers more realistic alternatives. After listing the important factors in making a decision, Tappan comes up with a solution: the small rural community.

> I remained convinced that only a community of reasonable size
> with a balance of vital skills would be both workable for the long
> term and proof against attack by the determined bands of well-
> organized looters which seem bound to emerge from the   crisis
> period.

Mel Tappan and Nancy Tappan acted on these beliefs; during the
late 1970s, they moved to a 70-acre farm near Rogue River, Oregon.
They lived there together and developed the property until Mel Tappan's death in 1980.

Nancy Tappan has remained on her farm since then. Through
her editing of the *Personal Survival Letter*, she has continued the
survival-oriented work which she and her husband did together; and
this work, as mentioned earlier, is influential among survivalists.
Nancy Tappan, unlike her husband, spends little time examining the

general survivalist issues — politics, economics, special technology. Instead, she puts most of her attention into developing more efficient methods of running a small farm. Speaking to Marv Wolf (from *Survive* magazine) recently, she spoke her mind about survivalism and subsistence farming.

> If there's a big economic crunch and there isn't any food, how are you going to survive? You can't kill everybody that comes to your door asking for food.... Eventually you're going to get killed yourself. And if everybody is out there in the woods with a rifle, how much game is there going to be? After a while there won't be any. I plan on running *PSL* articles that will give people the information they need to become self-sufficient.

It appears that people want this information and use what they acquire. Many survivalists indicate a desire to establish some sort of retreat. What forms do they take? Homesteads? Wilderness cabins? Traditional farms? Some of these retreats serve multiple purposes for the individuals or families owning them. Summer cabins and second homes fit into this category. among the *Directory* survivalists, for instance, NY5 owns a retreat, intends to purchase another, but nonetheless wants "to be prepared without totally 'retreating' at the present time..." Similarly, CA12 has a summer property in Montana.

Other survivalists specify what they call "retreats," but without going into detail. These appear to be parcels of undeveloped land. CA13 speaks of owning "prime 10 acres partially irrigated farmland with trees, creek, springs, ponds, and septic approvals in southern Oregon." FL4 owns property in Carter County, Tennessee, but doesn't seem to have done much with it. TX7 has access "to a friend's farm about 60 miles from Fort Worth." And AL1 intends to build on a "large farm" which he will eventually inherit. Then there are survivalists who have made a complete move to their retreat. For the most part, such retreats are fairly substantial farms, since the persons owning them strive for some degree of self-sufficiency. AR3, for example, says that he is "in the process of transferring most of what I have to a rural area," and that his intention is "subsistance (sic) agriculture." CA19 and his family have "lived on a farm for five years." Others in rural areas — KS1, KY2, MA1, and at least a dozen other survivalists mentioned in the *Directory* — have also established themselves on farms more or less permanently. Some were already farmers; others have moved in from cities. What they share is a sense that farming is not simply a livelihood, but a matter of survival.

At times, these concerns prompt survivalists to make preparations which differ little from nonsurvivalist activities. The previous
chapter mentioned an overlap between certain dimensions of the survival movement and part of the back-to-the-land movement; however,
this overlap is not simply a question of food production. What some
of these survivalists and non-survivalists do is to reject a whole urban
lifestyle which they consider dangerous. The anti-city feelings are intense. As SD2 put it following a visit to an unspecified eastern city:
'After seeing the real world, she (SD2's wife) wondered what these
social outcasts would have the balls to do when there was no law or
police." Others indicate their sense of vulnerability in the cities. OR2
speaks for many other survivalists when he says, "I always felt that
city life made me weak and unprepared to live off the land, if necessary." What many survivalists seek is therefore an alternative to this
weakness and lack of preparation.

Private farms are one such alternative; another is the group
farm. Here, too, the impulse resembles that of the back-to-the-landers,
but the results are more complex. "We left the city 10 years ago," explains OR1, because of "air, water, and people pollution. Expensive.
Rural property (is) the best investment. We prepared home-sites for
our friends to follow but they wouldn't leave city 'security'."
However, OR1 (husband and wife) went ahead anyway, figuring that
someone will join them eventually. They would welcome "our kind of
people as tenants, buyers, part of Corp., church, planned unit
development or just good neighbors." WA3 takes this a step further:

> Our interest is in creating a survival village based on self-
> reliance, cooperation, security, and community. We have a
> large, beautiful place all set to go in south-central Washington..
> .we have done all the paperwork that keeps peace with the
> bureaucracy...now we need people to join us and   make it
> happen!

This couple — Larry and Meg Letterman — apparently plan to
establish a place suitable both for "good times" and crisis. Their project is unusually ambitious. Having purchased over 1,000 acres of
land in Klickitat County, Washington, the Lettermans are now selling
five-acre parcels of land to persons who wish to help them build their
"survival village." Prices for land range from $8,000 to $18,000 per
parcel. The Lettermans have sold several dozen parcels thus far.
'We're just getting started,' said Meg Letterman when I spoke with
her about Ponderosa Village. A jovial woman of 62, she went on to ex-

plain that "Lots of people have planned to move here but haven't because they can't sell their present home."

The Lettermans want to set up a rural community "that will be not only secure, but a satisfying place to live" — one which will be satisfying "now, during whatever serious problems lie ahead, and 'after Doomsday.' " When I asked Meg Letterman what sorts of people had contacted her and her husband about the village, she told me, "Over a thousand — all kinds of people. I'd say their ages range from their twenties to well into the sixties." Backgrounds range "from professionals to migrant workers. Generally, they're well-educated, independent types." There's some racial variety in those who inquire; for the time being, however, those who have purchased land are "all WASPs." What are their reasons for wanting to move to the village? '- 'People have all kinds of reasons," she told me. "Some want to get back to the land, some think in terms of survivalism, some figure it's a combination — the two go together. You can't have survival without going back to the land." I asked her about specific concerns that there will be a nuclear war. She replied, "Quite a few are worried about this. One couple already out here is preparing for nuclear war and bacteriological war. Others are thinking about it. We (Meg and Larry Letterman) have dug the foundation to our home, and we'll build a fallout shelter. There's a variety of opinion. My husband and I figure that it's not likely to happen, but you should be prepared."

The result of these concerns already appears to be one of the most elaborate survivalist ventures in the country. Few survivalists would even attempt such a project, let alone attain it. Most strive for nothing more extensive than a few dozen acres of tillable land, a house, a fallout shelter, and supplies sufficient to keep things running. However, even those with modest intentions share at least the desire for relative self-sufficiency. "Our foremost aim is to become totally self-reliant," says AR2, and his fellow Arkansan in the *Directory* puts it this way: "I have the makings for general independence and more." Nearly a dozen survivalists listed in the *Directory* voice similar sentiments. CA19 and CA35, working separately, intend comparable levels of independence. Speaking of his plans, CA19 states that

My family and I have lived on a farm for five years, however my survival plans revolve around relocation...to a rugged, remote (nearest neighbor is eight miles away) mountain property which

I am currently developing near our home.... My preparation for
the future is predicated on self-sufficiency for a long time...
perhaps several generations.

These survivalists' ideal shelter is, in short, considerably more
than a current version of what people constructed in the 1950s. It
isn't simply a question of a *structure* — although blast and fallout
shelters enter into the overall scheme. Rather, it's a matter of a whole
context of beliefs, decisions, activities, and consequences which
change the survivalists' lives deeply and intricately. Shelter — to put
it bluntly — can be a matter of withdrawal from mainstream society.

Are these "retreaters" an extreme wing of the survival
movement? Are they the ideal to which other survivalists aspire?
What is the norm for survival shelter in the Eighties? A basement
bunker? A farm in Idaho? Both? And what trend seems likely if the
survival movement keeps growing?

The sheer range of beliefs and practices outlined in this chapter
should suggest that there is no single survivalist agenda when it comes
to shelter. *Survival* is the agenda; beyond that, opinions differ. Some
survivalists do, in fact, fit the stereotype of the mountain hermit. One
man wrote to me and explained that during two years in Alaska,   he
'saw humans 3 times,' and he wanted to keep it that way. At the other
end of the spectrum, survivalists like the Lettermans want to create a
community with more than superficial similarities to various utopian
endeavors. Most other alternatives occur between the extremes.
Shelter, like food storage, appears to engender any number of
responses.

It is worth noting, however, that this variety is controversial not
just outside of the survival movement, but within it as well. Options
for shelter amount to considerably more than an architectural sm-
orgasbord. One survivalist's wise preparations may look like sheer folly to another. For example, architect Joel Skousen regards the Terrene Ark project in Utah with nothing short of derision. "Anything
done in the commercial realm like that requires advertising," he told
me. "This makes it vulnerable. But the major flaw is that the design is
too conspicuous. Technically it's all right, but they've destroyed their
own security. There's nothing like a bunker door to make you conspicuous." He adds that, "People shouldn't even necessarily cut free
from society. It might be better for people living in L.A. to stay put,
for example."

In response, an advocate of rural retreats like Mel Tappan would criticize survivalists who make such recommendations. "Remaining in a city is totally out of the question," he wrote in *Tappan on Survival*, "and even living in a relatively out of the way place in an area of high overall population density is extremely hazardous." What he might have replied specifically to Skousen is uncertain; his general sentiments are not. As Bruce Clayton put it, "This (Skousen's) philosophy isn't too popular with the macho crowd." Kurt Saxon, as usual, is even more blunt on this issue: "There are some who call themselves Urban Survivalists but I consider that a contradiction in terms."

There are also some problems related to shelter which rivals within the movement might not acknowledge. One is simply expense. At a time when "the average American just can't afford to own a home these days" (according to Roy Green, chairman of the U.S. League of Savings Associations), how many can purchase a Biosphere Corporation fallout shelter — let alone a Terrene Ark condominium or one of Joel Skousen's $300,000 survival homes? Many survivalists argue, of course, that survival measures are a matter of priorities. It's the old Ant vs. Grasshopper argument again. Will you prepare for hard times or just fiddle your life away? As author Will Brownell states in his *Survive* magazine article on shelter (July/August, 1982), "A basic egg (shelter) package will cost from $14,000. Delivery and installation are variables that will add to the cost, but the total won't be much more than many people pay for a luxury automobile." This ignores the fact that most Americans can't afford either the shelter *or* the auto. As the folksong goes:

If livin' was a thing that money could buy, You know the rich would live and the poor would die.

Another (and even more basic) issue: is this sort of shelter really a shelter? Will it protect the people who take refuge in it? Of course, most of the data regarding fallout and blast are fairly straightforward. Nuclear tests have provided data which allow engineers to design suitable protection from most bombs under specific circumstances. Properly located and constructed, fallout shelters can limit their occupants' exposure to radiation with remarkable effectiveness. But what about other consequences of a nuclear war? What about damage to the ozone shield? What about other kinds of ecological disruptions? Will even the strongest, thickest, deepest bunker protect the people inside it from these side effects? Will even the most remote retreat escape them?

These questions, like those raised at the end of the previous chapter deserve special attention. Before attempting any answers, however, there is still one more aspect of the basic survivalist agenda which we must examine.

Chapter Five

Defense: "Peace through Superior Firepower"

A Story Problem (worth 10 points):

Jack and Sally Smith have organized a survival retreat with some friends in Idaho. When World War III breaks out, Jack and Sally meet nine of their friends at the retreat and take refuge in the fallout shelter. Some neighboring survivalists, however, who have their own retreat but no shelter, attack the Smith group: they want access to the shelter, and are willing to use deadly force to get it. The Smith group fights back.

The Smith group owns 8 BM-59 assault rifles, 3 SIG AMTs, 1 HK 91, and 2 Ruger Mini-14s; 4 High Standard Model 10B 12 ga. riot guns and 2 Remington 870 riot pump 12 ga. shotguns; 6 Colt .45 autopistols, 3 double action Model 29 S&W .44 Magnum double action revolvers, and 1 S&W Model 19 .357 Magnum; plus 10,823 rounds of assorted ammunition. The invaders number twelve persons — eight men and four women — and have a comparable battery of weapons.

...**Question:** at the end of the battle, how many survivalists are still alive?

Or to put the problem more directly: "But what do you do when outsiders try to barge in and steal your supplies or throw you out of your own shelter?'' as Bruce Clayton asks in *Life After Doomsday*. He responds: "The answer is obvious. You either let them have their way, or you oppose them." Whether or not the answer is "obvious," many survivalists do, in fact, tend to think in these either/or terms. It's the old Sixties bomb shelter dilemma in Eighties garb. Nothing is more controversial about the survival movement — or, for that matter, within it.

The various theoreticians are divided on this issue. Howard Ruff, for instance, claims in *How to Prosper During the Coming Bad Years*, that "I have never advocated that you have an armed retreat in the mountains with an arsenal to kill the 'attacking hordes.' " Cresson Kearny goes a step further in *Nuclear War Survival Skills*: "Some maintain that after an atomic attack America would degenerate into anarchy — and every-man-for-himself struggle for existence. They forget...the self-sacrificing strengths most human beings are capable of displaying." He plainly advocates cultivating these strengths.

> Like the heroic Russians who drove food trucks to starving Leningrad through bursting Nazi bombs and shells, many Americans would risk radiation and other dangers to bring truckloads of grain and other necessities to their starving countrymen. Surely, an essential part of psychological preparations for surviving a modern war is a well-founded assurance that many citizens will struggle to help each other and will work together with little regard for danger and loss.

Other writers take a harder line. Bruce Clayton states that "I feel that I have a moral obligation to warn people of the troubled times ahead and show them how to prepare themselves, but once they have been warned, I feel no further obligation..." What are the consequences of this ethical stance? "If you refuse to share your supplies," he continues, "on the grounds that you have only enough to save yourself and family, are you justified in using force to protect those supplies? I think you are fully justified.... The principle of self-defense clearly applies." He proceeds to elaborate on subjects like "Selecting Your Defense Arsenal," "Firearm Accessories," "Defense of a Fixed Position," and "Defense of Moving Vehicles." Clayton's discussions seem like *How to Win Friends and Influence People* compared to those of other survivalist manuals. Kurt Saxon's newsletter, *The Survivalist*, advocates preparation for violent encounters.

Unlike the back-to-the-landers, the ecologists, the retreaters and such, survivalists are not non-involved pacifists.... They are simply aware that civilization is cracking up and see the possible need for desperate measures to come through with a whole skin.... When the worst is over you might have seen some turmoil and even driven away some urban marauders. But you and yours will survive with dignity and with no regrets.

The Weaponeer, another Saxon magazine, is even more explicit:

The Weaponeer will detail improvised weaponry in the finest tradition of *The Poor Man's James Bond* (Saxon's manual of "improvised weaponry and do-it-yourself mayhem"). Regardless of the availability of conventional weaponry you can feel secure.

You will be able to defend your home and loved ones with the most outrageous infernal gagetry (sic) imaginable. Your territory will be a nightmare of boobytraps, mines and alarm devices...

We will take no moral stance. We will leave moral considerations up to the individual.

Saxon's first issue of this publication includes articles entitled "Survival Shooting," "Mines and Booby Traps," "Unconventional Warfare Devices and Techniques," and "The Nasal Sprayer as a Weapon."

The most influential advocate of survival weapons, however, is unquestionably Mel Tappan. Other experts may be more generally or specifically trained; they may or may not share Tappan's survivalist orientation; but none has become so prominent to "gun guru" within the movement. Although educated primarily in other areas — university teaching, investment, corporate finance, and more recently survival theory — Tappan received the most attention for his book *Survival Guns* and the program of personal self-defense which it encourages. *Tappan on Survival,* a posthumous collection of magazine columns, has extended this influence.

Tappan's basic premise, like that of many survivalists, is that modern Americans have relinquished too much control over their own lives, and are consequently vulnerable to disruptions or even collapse of the culture as a whole. Also like other survivalists, he regarded moving out of cities and other potentially unstable areas to be an outright necessity. His recommendations differed from those of other survival consultants and writers primarily in a stress on acquiring specific weapons. "Whether you anticipate a calamity of some sort or whether you merely want to enjoy the satisfactions of a simple, rural life," he wrote in *Survival Guns*, "you will almost certainly have to deal with the realities of seclusion." There are two reasons for this, according to Tappan:

> Depending upon how isolated your retreat is and whether mass social disorders become a reality, trips to the supermarket will fall somewhere between inconvenient and impossible. You will have to provide at least a substantial portion of your own food. Again, depending upon your location and the prevailing social conditions, you may be threatened by intruders and the nearest help may be miles away — if it is there at all.

Since Tappan believed social upheaval and nuclear war to be likely events during the next few decades, and since he expected violence to spread in their aftermath, he therefore urged careful planning of a survivalist's defense strategy.

> No other purchase which you might make in preparation for your survival — with the possible exception of your retreat itself — is likely to have as much to do with whether you stay alive as your survival battery. Unless you are willing to settle for minimum survival odds, do not skimp on you selection of firearms.

Discounting what he called "Daniel Boone romanticism," Tappan then proceeded to recommend a wide variety of weapons, each designated for specific purposes. "I am going to suggest," he wrote, "that your survival battery include two separate categories of guns: defense and working (those suitable for hunting and pest control) and that neither should be expected to do double duty." Some of these are guns easily found throughout rural America — shotguns, sporting rifles, and so forth. Others are less common. In *Tappan on Survival*, he wrote that

> At a rural retreat or on an isolated farm in the aftermath of conditions which this column contemplates...a suitable defense rifle should be regarded as the single most important element in any survival battery.
> If such events do occur, you are likely to encounter a superior force of armed rabble looting and burning everything in its path, and if you are to have a reasonable chance of

defending yourself and your family, you are going to need more than casual arms and indifferent skills. Let's be clear on this point. Your deer rifle, a surplus GI carbine, or a menacing looking short rifle using pistol ammunition is simply not adequate under these circumstances. You will need absolutely reliable firepower at a high level — the ability to deliver disabling hits rapidly a reasonably long ranges without sufficient interruptions.

Tappan recognized that some people would find his recommendations upsetting, and consequently tried to pre-empt their criticism.

At the risk of being thought an alarmist (he wrote in *Survival Guns*) I must point out that if we have a serious social breakdown in this country, there could be mass desertion by the armed forces and police, together with widespread looting of military bases, National Guard and police arsenals. Logically, the large number of sophisticated and highly efficient fighting weapons which they contain will end up in the hands of looters. You may, therefore, one day find yourself being attacked by determined adversaries armed with automatic weapons, grenades, mortars, tear gas and even flame throwers. In such an event, the very best defensive weapons you can have will be none too good.

Tappan concludes *Survival Guns* with ten example batteries which fit his recommendations for particular survival groups and families. Battery No. 1, for instance — designed for a married couple in their thirties — includes six handguns, three assault rifles, and three shotguns for the "defense" function; five handguns, seven rifles, and five shotguns for the "working" function; plus five rimfire (specialized .22 caliber) pistols, eight rimfire rifles, four other miscellaneous guns, one hunting bow with arrows, a crossbow with bolts, two Argentine *bolas*, and "assorted slingshots." This, according to Tappan, is nearly "a dream battery," though earlier he describes it as having "no frills." The point, he says, is to "approach the selection of your survival battery without romantic illusions — as if it were a stark, pressing matter of life or death. It may be just that."

To what extent are survivalists willing to act on this sort of information? It's hard to tell. The notorious reticence among survivalists is probably at its most intense when the subjects of weapons and defense come up. Many won't answer questions; others evade them. Whether this unwillingess to talk indicates preparation or lack of it is uncertain, and probably varies from person to person. One thing seems clear: most people intent on protecting their survival supplies wouldn't boast too specifically about how they figure on doing it.

My conversations and correspondence with survivalists have provided various sorts of information on the subject, though erratically. For the most part, I find that survivalists hesitate to talk about their weapons more than they do regarding any other subject; and those who stock the most elaborate armories seem the wariest of all. (The exceptions are "self-appointed vigilantes waving machine guns," as Bruce Clayton puts it: the media-hounds which most members of the survival movement condemn. Nonetheless, some people are as willing to discuss this subject as any other.

One survivalist who has spoken with me at length went into detail about his defense preparations. "The question of defense is certainly a soul-searching one. For those who are not willing to defend themselves, their families might team up with someone who will. The taking of another life is a very soul-rending decision for most people and the slightest hesitation on one's part could mean the difference between life and death. Having been in Viet Nam, I would not hesitate to defend myself and my family by whatever means necessary." Regarding other survivalists, he expresses a common opinion: "Those survivalists I am familiar with would not hesitate to defend themselves. Unfortunately, some are extremely militaristic and are almost looking forward to using their 'skills.' Fortunately, they are in the minority. Unfortunately, they are the ones who seem to get all the publicity."

Another survivalist — a Californian in his early sixties — expressed a similar worry: in the aftermath of a nuclear war, "There would be armed bands up here." Like others, he feels a need to be prepared for them. He has taught his wife and children how to use firearms. "We're moderately well-prepared to defend ourselves," he said. A young physician who practices in central Indiana shares this attitude. He told me, "Any prudent person would be justified in defending himself after a disaster." He received weapons training in the Army, considers guns to be "very dangerous," but has nonetheless purchased a rifle and a handgun for his wife's and his own use.

Others have some unusual opinions about weapons. A Marine Corps sergeant, for instance, told me that despite his knowledge of guns, he regards them as inadequate. "During a time of crisis, it's doubtful that ammo manufacturers and shipping concerns will continue operating, except for the government — if any. It follows that there will be a limited supply of ammunition for the average citizen. Now, I realize that assault rifles and combat guns in general are great offensive and defensive tools, but what are these survivalists going to do when they run out of ammo? Beat the bad guys with the butt of their weapon? Perhaps bayonet them? Hogwash!" And so he suggests this solution to the problem: "I know from personal experience that a man with a good sword, pike, axe, etc., can maneuver more rapidly and effectively, provided he is familiar with their use, than an expert with a bayonet on his rifle, and consistently defeat said rifle-bearing fool. The swordsman has reach, balance, thrust range, and momentum over the rifleman." In addition to ease of use, the sergeant recommended swords for another reason. "If you want to take someone else's stuff — food, clothing, women, animals, etc. — why wake the entire population when you start your attack? You can eliminate sentries silently and effectively if you cut their head off, and everybody else continues sleeping peacefully. You can be halfway done and no losses to your side before they realize that something is amiss."

For the most part, however, survivalists' attitudes seem fairly conventional. Bruce Clayton's *Survivalist Directory* gives some interesting indications of trends within the movement. Clayton himself makes only the most general interpretations of his data regarding personal defense:

> Part of the myth of the survivalist fostered by news magazines and TV programs in that survivalists are all gun nuts. In my experience survivalists are very cautious and concerned about one another's attitudes toward the use of lethal force in a survival situation. Therefore, I decided to ask a leading question about guns. Some respondents turned out to be enthusiastic pro-gun collectors and shootists, but most people seemed to regard guns either as tools or as unpleasant necessitities.

All in all, I agree with this assessment; but it's worth noting, too, that one person's responsible marksman is another's "gun nut," and vice versa. There are complex ethical issues involved here which go beyond stereotypes of the sort which Clayton mentions. (When, for instance, is self-defense justifiable? When someone attacks you?

When they merely threaten to attack? When they threaten to take your survival food?) In any case, the fact remains that of Clayton's 161 respondents, 113 made explicit or implicit mention of owning guns, and another six made ambiguous statements about ownership. Only three stated outright that they do not own guns; one of those said so with regret. Another made a vague comment about guns being "too available."

The basic survivalist position in Clayton's *Directory* is this: guns are a necessity. Some of these survivalists considered preparations to be not just for the future, but necessary even now. "Where we live," said CA5, "motorcycle gangs drive past nearly every day, but the Sheriff is 25 minutes away and the phones don't always work. We don't dwell on the possibility of violence, but we know it is there." CA35 has more of an eye for the future: "I feel that proper weapons are an integral part of any preparedness situation for personal defense and hunting." Much in the same vein, NY5 (female, 35) states that "I believe in the use of firearms for self-defense and the protection of one's property and family. In a 'survival' situation, I would not hesitate to condone or use weapons as necessary." AR1 (also a woman) puts it more bluntly: "With everyone in the world possessing (guns) it's like asking, 'How do I feel about a smallpox vaccination?' You'd better have yours, too."

Most of these people indicate not only a willingness to own weapons, but to use them as well. (This may seem self-evident; however, some survivalists spoke of hoping that weapons would serve as a "deterrent.") TX12 wrote that "I would not kill a fellow man for food but would not hesitate if lives were endangered to use any force necessary to counter the threat." MO1 was more emphatic: "...aggressive action toward our person or property or those we are grouped with by lawless, rebellious persons would be dealt with swiftly and severely." Likewise for CA15: "Persons attempting to harm my loved ones, myself, or my supplies will have committed inadvertant (sic) suicide." The implications of such comments are not simply a fear of "marauders" or "the starving hordes." Survivalists generally worry that a nuclear disaster would send mobs of refugees their way, and that they would have to fend them off; but there is also an implicit fear of another element. After all, some survivalists intend more than just defensive use of weapons. OH7, for instance, seems concerned about "radical survivalists who own an arsenal and are waiting for an opportunity to use it." MA1, though a weapons expert,   criticized 'clowns who only stock guns and ammo and plan to take everything else they need. They'll be a bigger handicap than an asset.' And CA18 went into more detail:

> There are many people out there who are living it up right now with no regard to their future that will think nothing of robbing you if that is the only way they can put food on their table...

Of all the *Directory* respondents, 72 stated explicitly or implicitly that they would we willing to kill someone if necessary. (I'm considering a statement like "I would not hesitate to kill" to be about as explicit as anyone would want; and I consider a comment like, "I believe all family members could defend self and property" to be implicit.)

In contrast, twenty-four indicated qualms of one sort or another about killing. These ranged from strong moral qualms — "Life is precious and should not be taken without due justification" (CT1) to unusual standards — "I would be much less reluctant to use guns against a human attacker than an innocent animal" (CA20) — to vague ambivalence — "Survival should not depend on guns, but guns have there (sic) place in ultimate defense." CA9, for instance, said that "I would only be willing to use guns as a last resort to protect myself and those around me after all else fails." MI2 expressed the same sort of hesitance and criteria for overcoming it: "I hate the thought of taking a life, but if a person is trying to steal from me or take my life, I won't hesitate to defend myself by any means necessary." Approximately twelve others in the *Directory* made similar statements. Others mention more specific reservations. "We are planning to purchase guns..." said MD2. "I still have mixed feelings on killing others to protect myself, but will have to resolve that question before the situation arises." Though willing to defend himself, CA19 nonetheless stated that "I cannot envisage killing my neighbor."

Clayton himself sums up the response by explaining that:

> Nearly everyone said that they would use lethal force in self-defense if they or their families were threatened, and many people extended this position to cover stockpiled food as well. Quite a number of people made the explicit distinction that they would fight if attacked but would never consider murdering or robbing their neighbor... One or two felt that they would be justified in

taking what they needed at gunpoint if it would keep their
families from starving. One person longed for more effective
gun control. In contrast, most people made strong anti-control
statements on the Constitutional right to keep and bear arms.

There's another aspect of personal defense, however, which we
should examine before trying to make sense of the whole picture. This
is the existence of "survival groups." Although individuals and
families may band together for various reasons — sharing expenses,
pooling skills, or just keeping each other company — the most prominent is probably defense. It's an old story. Since prehistoric times,
human beings have sought each other not simply out of
gregariousness, but also because numbers mean safety.

Defense groups are actually as controversial within the movement as other aspects of the general issue of defense. Mel Tappan
argues against them if the group is a communal arrangement; as usual,
his opinions have influenced many survivalists. He argues in *Tappan
on Survival* that:

> ...group retreats sound good in theory but once you begin in-
> vesting actual examples, serious problems become apparent.
> There are too many rules and regulations, or too few; there is
> great difficulty in getting balance of needed skills in a group...
> Whether utopias or group retreats, artificial communities have a
> tendency not to work out.

His arguments seem plausible. Tappan argued instead for the
security of a small town. However, many survivalists find the attrac-
tions of cooperative retreats more persuasive, and groups appear to be
proliferating.

Bruce Clayton's *Directory* gives an indication of the interest level.
"About 70 entries are from people looking for a group to join.
Another 30 are from groups looking for additional people. A lot of
people are looking for allies in the fight for survival and don't know
how to reach them." Considering that the *Directory* contains 161
listings, the 100 or so respondents in some way interested in groups is
significant. (The response, however, is skewed, since the *Directory*
serves essentially as a kind of survivalist "dating service" anyway.
Clayton himself admits this. "Unquestionably," he says, "this is the
reason for existence of the Directory.")

Not all of those persons interested in groups necessarily seek them because of the defense issue, but those who do are nonetheless remarkably frank about their concerns and needs. TX10, for instance, states that his biggest problem is "...self-defense. We are limited to the number of people in our family which presents problems when it comes to defense on a long-term basis." He therefore wished to hear from "like-minded people in this area. Ideally I would like to have several families united for mutual protection." FL1 wants to find individuals or families to form a group, but specifies that he prefers "association with those not afraid to use deadly force in the protection of themselves and their survival community." CA18, who wants to move to eastern Oregon or Washington, argues that "Any person who doesn't have guns and know how to use them is just wasting his time..." and he adds that "...a good selection of guns is your best insurance to keep what you have."

The survivalists among my own contacts indicate similar concerns. One survivalist — a man who identifies himself only as "Evil" — has told me about his reasons for joining what he calls a "survival squad." Citing concerns about nuclear war and a "Russian-like dictatorship," Evil explained that "I became a vigilante to not only take care of myself, but others not able to. I joined a more or less local survival group. It was easy to join; I knew some members. It was *too* easy, I thought. I could have been someone trying to expose them. We mainly met at a 'hideaway,' I'll call it, to discuss what we should do, and when. There was much talk of hoarding and defending the store against others. Fine stuff. But all talk. When I myself suggested we train for this day, or donate money to buy equipment, it was 'I don't have time now, but I'll be ready, don't worry,' Bullshit!"

Evil therefore "...quit and started my own survivalist squad. That's right — squad. You see, I not only wanted to prepare for forthcoming days of 'bad weather,' as my squad calls it, but also assist in matters that chickenshits, policemen, and the law cannot, or will not, aid in. My survival squad is taking members only by application — kept on file only by me — that are carefully scrutinized. We want no possible leaks. We employ disciplinary action and even banishment as a deterrent to publicity. Much of what we do does not come within the limits of the law." When asked about specific activities, Evil has been unwilling to explain further. He does, however mention "regular training for various emergency situations," and he states that "our vigilantes have fought in several riots as much as one hundred miles away from home base."

Another militant survivalist group is the Wapaloosie Mountain National Survival Base. This group, located in northeastern Washington State, is primarily a local organization, but its founder, Jim Watkins, implies that some or all members take part in broader-based survivalist activities. (More on national groups below.) "Soon we will begin training and classes on different important subjects of survival," Watkins told me recently. These subjects include some which concern nuclear war. "I feel we, the American people, are headed for nuclear confrontation or a political peace definitely not favorable to our freedom. If such a war comes, we will be *very* hard put to survive, but I believe it can be done and it is worth doing so." Watkins has been reluctant to describe his activities in detail; but the form of survivalism he advocates includes "forming a militia unit," and he states that "this is the catagory of survivalism I fit in."

In addition to small, individual groups scattered throughout the United States, there are also a number of national survivalist organizations, and some of these focus primarily on the issue of defense. Two aiming for widespread membership are Live Free, Inc., based in Harvey, Illinois, and the Christian-Patriots Defense League, with headquarters in Flora, Illinois.

Live Free, Inc., claims to be "America's fastest growing survival organization," and now has over 700 members throughout the country. James C. Jones, founder and president of the group, expresses the standard survivalist worries. "When things break down, any major city is going to be bad news," he said recently. If you are planning on staying in a large city until disaster strikes, choose something at least 100 miles from any major city." Jones and some of his followers have consequently purchased 39 acres of land near Baraboo, Wisconsin — their retreat in case suburban Chicago comes under attack. Preparations include not only stockpiling of supplies, but also training and practice drills. Jones explains, "We try to be practical. We don't think it makes sense to quit our jobs and move out of the cities. So we practice on weekends." During these weekend drills, Live Free members work on their marksmanship and even go through mock invasions: one squad attacks the camp while another holds off the intruders.

The Christian-Patriots Defense League, meanwhile, is an even more militant group. Along with its two sister organizations — the Christian Conservative Churches of America and the Citizens Emergency Defense System — the C-PDL advocates "the total destruction of International Communism, along with the forces and powers behind it...regardless of cost or consequences, and by whatever means required or necessary." These groups have various agendas, including some which are not specifically survivalist (such as removal of the United States from the UN); but other concerns fall within the scope of the survival movement. John R. Harrell, founder of the C-PDL, writes in a pamphlet called *The Golden Triangle* that "We are now in a headlong rush to global judgement and absolute slavery, death and oblivion," and, that "nuclear war shall fulfill the Bible prophecy of flesh falling from the bones and eyes dropping from sockets as recorded in the 14th chapter of Zechariah and elsewhere." Like Jim McKeever and other fundamentalist Christian survivalists, he therefore urges true believers to "prepare for the storm."

C-PDL recommendations are not simply theoretical, however. This organization sponsors "Freedom Festivals" which include workshops on various aspects of survivalism. For instance, the 1982 Festival, held in Louisville, Illinois, in June, included workshops entitled Defense, Archery and Crossbow, Guns and Reloading, Knife Fighting, Guard Dog Training, Nuclear Weapons and Radiation, Marksmanship, Demolition and Camouflage, Anti-Aircraft and Anti-Tank, and Street Action. A *Time* magazine article by Dennis Morrison (November 5, 1979) described an earlier C-PDL freedom Festival.

> Barrett (a C-PDL instructor) is ripe with other combat wisdom: "If you bring (an enemy) down, don't run up to him so he can shoot you back. Give him time to die... When things break down there's going to be an initial surge of people from the cities. They'll kill you for a can of sardines... You should band together with a few families, because you're going to need all the firepower you can get. If you have a nine- or ten-year-old kid, teach him how to shoot...

So what does all this amount to? The current stereotype of a survivalist shows us a camouflage-clad gun fanatic armed to the eyebrows. Survivalists themselves, resenting this cliche, often insist that members of the movement are considerably more than just a pack of "shootists." (Some even claim that survivalists are in fact more responsible than their non-survivalist neighbors. As a Live Free, Inc., leaflet says: "THE MOST DANGEROUS PEOPLE IN AMERICA TODAY ARE THE NONSURVIVALISTS. Every person who has not made provisions for surviving without food, water, fuel and other essential needs from the outside, is a mortal danger to his neighbors.")

Where does the truth lie? Or is the truth — as in other aspects of survivalism — scattered all over the place? At the extremes *and* in the middle?

Some observers have tried to explain the issue of defense by making a distinction between "soft-core" and "hard-core" survivalists. Soft-core survivalists are those who address all the various survival issues except personal defense; or at least their means of addressing it (such as secretive activities) does not involve the use of guns. Hard-core survivalists, on the other hand, are more militant. They acquire weapons and are willing to use them.

As with all dichotomies, the hard-core/soft-core classification risks being too simplistic. It suggests that the degree of a survivalist's commitment is proportional to his willingness to use weapons — a questionable proposition. Some of the most elaborately prepared survivalists scarcely consider themselves members of the survival movement, let alone "hard-core," and they may not own any guns at all. In contrast, some of the most heavily armed survivalists have done little but amass their weapons; other survivalists spurn them as irresponsible pseudo-members, pariahs, pirates. The hard-core/soft-core distinction also fails to mark off gradations of concern for personal defense and differences among various sorts of gun-related activity.

One writer who has suggested an alternate scheme for interpreting the issue of defense in Bruce Clayton. Writing in the *Journal of Civil Defense* (August, 1981), Clayton states that "much of the controversy about survivalism hinges on the image of the gun-toting radical who talks about 'shooting neighbors.' The actual situation is a little different." He explained this situation to me: "The hard-core/soft-core categories are an oversimplification," he said. "There are four categories, maybe five."

"The first category is the people who wouldn't want to have any guns at all. I call them *Mother Earth News* subscribers. They'd probably deny they're even survivalists." The second group, according to Clayton, is the group of "survivalists who are storing food and watching their investments, but don't really express any interest in the books and such. I call them Ruff Readers." These people, too, most likely have no guns. (Appearances in this regard can be deceptive. Howard Ruff promotes himself as reluctant to encourage defense-related activity, but in fact he owns guns and implies intention to use them; and he says as much in his *How to Prosper During the Coming Bad Years*.)

Categories three through five are those generally considered "hard-core." Clayton notes the differences between them. The third category is made up of "people with 'working guns' — tools of the trade — like a rancher or a chicken farmer. Maybe they use them for varmint control." These people, in short, own guns almost coincidentally to their survival preparations. Guns are simply a part of what many farmers and ranchers consider "ordinary" survival measures. In the fourth category, however, "there are those with working guns plus combat rifles. The reason is this (and you have to be careful so you don't sound too paranoid): in case of a nuclear attack, the phones won't be working. Therefore, if you need protection, you're on your own." Clayton elaborates on this situation in his *Journal of Civil Defense* article:

> I think that a person like myself who possesses a fallout shelter and a year's supply of food and medicine might perhaps be excused for brooding on the possibility that one dark day a desperate mob might try to take advantage of my foresight by force of arms. This is the common nightmare of everyone who has prepared for a nuclear attack. I don't like being in this position, but I feel trapped into it by my responsibility to my family and the negligence of the government and the population in general to adequately prepare for nuclear war survival.

He goes on to say that "there is another reason why I own these firearms, and why I have learned to use them skillfully. The reason is the shoot-'em-up crowd" — the fifth group of survivalists. "They say they're survivalists," Clayton told me, "but they don't have any food." Clayton considers them no more than marauders. "They own substantial stockpiles of guns, ammunition, and other military supplies...but no food! They plan to survive by preying on others, like the Mexican bandits of the Old West. We legitimate survivalists want nothing to do with them." The reason, he continued, is not simply that "the most vocal" of them "are frequently very extreme politically, very racist." It is also a matter of these marauders' threat not only to the general public, but to survivalists in particular. "Think about it. The only people the marauders can take from (after a nuclear disaster) would be other survivalists. Nobody else is going to have food. When you ask people where they'll get food, they say 'I figure I'll get it from you.' "

Clayton's deepest worry about personal defense is therefore not even the danger of "starving neighbors," but rather the risk of these well-armed marauders. "Some of them must be making 'shopping lists' for places to hit up — where to go looking for the goodies. Some of them are even running combat schools — 'consultants in defense.' This allows them to identify and locate other survivalists. They'll know you're spending money; they may know if you have food; and they'll know, whatever else, that you're armed and how good you are."

Regardless of whether Clayton's categories (or any others) delineate the limits of one group from another, the basic fact is that personal defense is a matter of great concern for most survivalists. The concern appears to be growing. Some survivalists deny having guns, and it is possible that most of them are telling the truth; on the other hand, some of the most unassuming individuals turn out to own huge arsenals. Perhaps the only generalization possible right now is that many survivalists have acquired weapons. This trend also appears to be growing.

It's worth noting that the controversy over defense, like other aspects of survivalism, is nothing new. The civil defense fad of the 1960s also sparked an intense debate about weapons and the possibility that someone would use them against fellow-citizens. Owners of fallout shelters claimed the right to fight off ill-prepared neighbors in the event of a nuclear attack; other citizens argued against what they considered a frontier mentality. During the height of the Sixties shelter boom, magazines and newspapers added their own opinions — articles with titles like "Gun They Neighbor?" and "The Shelter and the Shotgun." According to *Time* magazine (August 18, 1961), a hardware dealer named Charles Davis "stashed four rifles and a .357 Magnum pistol in his shelter" and threatened to use them if necessary. The public response was widespread outrage. Another man, a Chicago suburbanite, said, "When I get my shelter finished, I'm going to mount a machine gun at the hatch to keep the neighbors out if the bomb falls. I'm deadly serious about this." He justified his intentions by arguing that "If the stupid American public will not do what they have to to save themselves, I'm not going to run the risk of not being able to use the shelter I've taken the trouble to provide...my own family."

In short, the ethical issues — self-defense vs. condemnation of armed force — seem to have stayed the same during the past twenty years. What has definitely changed is the technology involved. Personal defense is no longer a question of a shotgun or several sporting rifles. Those who believe that weapons ensure safety ("Peace Through Superior Firepower," according to a popular slogan) frequently own weapons of astonishing power and sophistication. Like the proponents of nuclear deterrence, they feel confident that the mere threat of deadly force prevents a need to use it.

Although the outcome of such confidence remains unsure, one thing seems certain: a war, a depression, or even another oil embargo would heighten the tensions between rich and poor, black and white, rural folks and urbanites; the defense issue raises the stakes, intensifies the resentments, and increases the dangers to everyone. Even the term "defense" is sometimes a misnomer. Some of the arsenals that survivalists have acquired seem worthy of private armies. A group called the Church of the White Seed, for instance, which has survivalist orientations, has reportedly acquired over $47,000 worth of small-arms ammunition in northern Wisconsin; presumably they own the weapons to match. Bruce Clayton tells of at least a few survivalists who stock hand grenades and others who even own an armored personnel carrier.

The implications disturb even (especially?) committed survivalists like Clayton. Despite his worries about nuclear war, he sometimes seems less concerned about living through a possible holocaust than about coexisting with fellow survivalists. A group organized for communal safety might find itself violently divided in the heat of a crisis. Few survivalists seem to examine the wider consequences of their actions. One who does is Lane Blackmore: speaking of his Terrene Ark I, he told me, "People may have their own weapons (while residing there), but we suggest that they (the weapons) be put into our central armory. The effects of stress might produce mishaps."

Aside from the ethical issues here — as if they *can* be set aside — the practical ones make the whole matter ludicrous: too many survivalists seem intent on parodying the arms race which got us into this mess in the first place. The ultimate irony would be if these people survive the doomsday they anticipate but end up killing each other in its aftermath.

Chapter Six

Survivalism and Civil Defense

If any one situation has prompted the survival movement, it is the lack of a popular civil defense program in the United States. Of course, many circumstances generate survivalist activities: economic problems, rising crime rates, risks of war, and any number of phenomena which Americans in general fear and resent. Even specific courses of action — the building of fallout shelters, for instance — can originate from a variety of political, social, and cultural attitudes. Still, it appears unlikely that survivalists would be as numerous or as earnest as they are, had the U.S. government taken more extensive civil defense preparations.

The survivalists themselves are often emphatic in this regard. Cresson Kearny, for instance, though involved with civil defense programs during most of his long career, lambasts current American policy as inadequate, irresponsible, and even immoral. Criticizing the nuclear strategy of Mutually Assured Destruction (MAD), Kearny writes in *Nuclear War Survival Skills* that "As long as MAD for all practical purposes is our governing policy, most Americans will remain unprotected hostages to the Soviet (sic) Union." Kearny advocates that citizens pressure the American government into abandoning this policy and promoting civil defense instead. "Only then," he says, "will effective civil defense preparations be made an important part of U.S. capabilities to maintain peace through strength, or to save tens of millions from death if deterrence fails and nuclear war strikes." Since government officials seem unwilling or unable to undertake a comprehensive program, however, Kearny feels that the best hope for the Americans to survive a nuclear attack "is for private organizations to make widely available field-tested, do-it-yourself instructions...and for concerned citizens to use these instructions to the best of their abilities."

Other writers take an even stronger stand. Thomas Nieman argues in *Better "Read" Than Dead*, that "this responsibility (civil defense) has been minimized and virtually ignored by the successive administrations over the past 20 years... Civil survival has undergone innumerable public debates...with nothing positive forthcoming." But he objects to more than just governmental inaction. Nieman also criticizes what he considers to be ineffectual or counterproductive civil defense plans. For example, Nieman faults the Federal Emergency Management Agency (FEMA) for promulgating its Crisis Relocation Plan. (CRP) that involves evacuating U.S. cities in time of nuclear crisis and relocating urban residents in neighboring towns and rural areas. It is doubtful (according to Nieman) that CRP "could handle the population in the event of a real emergency." To put it bluntly, "The result of a Crisis Relocation Program (sic) being carried out will result in the world's longest and last traffic jam."

Nieman, like Kearny, therefore advocates taking the civil defense bull by the horns. "Key persons from all over this great land must meet to join in and lead the fight for survival NOW, he states. "Hundreds and thousands of people and businesses all across the United States could join together, along with government leadership, towards the establishment of a free enterprise system of civil defense." This could include builders, designers, architects, engineers, suppliers, and others able to guide citizens in this endeavor. Nieman's stress throughout is on individual effort. He states outright: "The only person you can depend on is YOURSELF."

Ultimately, the opinion of Kearny and Nieman imply the need for something like the survival movement. Lack of public programs (according to this view) justifies, and even *requires*, private endeavor. Kearny and Nieman are explicit in this regard; other survivalists theoreticians, however, share these sentiments, as do the rank and file survivalists. Bruce Clayton mentions several persons in his *Survivalist Directory* who express their resentment of inadequate civil defense. Writing about OH7, Clayton states that "he considers the U.S. Civil

Defense System (sic) a farce," and that "he expects to have to go it alone." PA2 is even more hostile about the situation. "He left his profession as an accountant and became a survivalist four years ago after learning of the gigantic nuclear war shelters our leaders have provided for themselves while leaving the rest of us defenseless," Clayton writes. "The mental vision of a world where the only survivors were politicians moved him to action." And CA26 indicates that he became a survivalist because of "our lack of civil defense. I checked out the county CD office. We have nothing. Plan nothing. The US government has no plans to instruct the population in nuclear survival. The only government plan is to relocate people out of big cities. This looks like a sure disaster."

It's important to note, however, that survivalists usually are not objecting to the general concept of civil defense, but rather to specific plans. Their chief objection to current American policy is that the absence of adequate programs not only jeopardizes the safety of Americans in general, but also doubles the jeopardy for survivalists. The Crisis Relocation Plan draws heavy fire in this regard. If urban Americans evacuate their cities at a time of crisis and relocate in neighboring towns and rural areas, the influx of "refugees" would end up precisely where many survivalists have also sought refuge. Current CRP contingencies do not provide for food, water, or sanitation facilities; refugees must make their own provisions. A CRP evacuation would unquestionably place heavy burdens on host communities. Survivalists therefore resent the personal risks which this program intensifies for them.

How survivalists respond to the situation varies considerably. Before examining these responses, though, we should examine actual civil defense policy in the United States and elsewhere; we should consider the implications of various programs; and we should also delineate the differences between civil defense and survivalism.

Responding to the risk of nuclear war, several western nations have undertaken extensive civil defense programs. Sweden, for instance, maintains a Civil Defense Administration, which in turn manages three interrelated programs: the Control and Warning System, the Protection and Evacuation System, and the Rescue System. These three programs cover peacetime as well as wartime threats. Preparation for possible nuclear attack includes extensive construction and maintainance of blast/fallout shelters. According to *Protect and Survive Monthly*, a British civil defense journal, "Shelters are situated in such a way as to allow the every day life of the population to continue with as little disturbance as possible in a state of emergency... Today Sweden has space for 5.5 million persons in its shelters, with new room being built for an additional 200,000 persons each year." The population of Sweden is currently eight million people; hence the Swedes have provided civil defense shelters for almost three-fourths of their countrymen. Shelters protect "against shock waves, splinters, the impact of collapsing structures, fires and radiation as well as against chemical and bacteriological weapons" (*Protect and Survive Monthly, February, 1982.*)

Similarly, Norway has undertaken a civil defense program which provides blast/fallout shelters for "nearly 2 million" persons — approximately 70% of the urban population (*Protect and Survive Monthly, December, 1981.*) Shelters provide varying degrees of protection against blast, radiation, and contaminated air. The Norwegian government has also made plans for evacuating some forty urban areas of the country. In addition, the government requires many industrial enterprises to build shelters for their employees. Some firms must even make shelters accessible to non-employees from neighboring areas (*Journal of Civil Defense*, April, 1981).

But Switzerland is unquestionably the western nation with the most elaborate and extensive civil defense program. According to Nigel Calder (writing in *Nuclear Nightmares*, Penguin Books, 1981), "Every new house in Switzerland must have a shelter in its foundation — and not merely an improvised fallout shelter." The Swiss government is strict about the necessary designs: "The law requires a strong structure with massive sealed doors and an air-filtration system, built to government specifications that make it resistant to the blast from a one-metaton H-bomb at a distance of 1.6 miles." As a result of these regulations, "four million Swiss had places in modern shelters and another 1.8 million could be accomodated in older shelters; altogether 90 percent of the Swiss population had protection of one sort or another. The aim is to have bed space in a modern shelter for every citizen. Switzerland also maintains emergency hospitals; there are currently more than seventy thousand hospital beds and a thousand operating rooms underground, according to Calder.

American advocates of extensive civil defense point to these European programs as models for what the United States could implement. These nations, they say, are unwilling to leave their citizens vulnerable to nuclear blackmail. (Switzerland receives the greatest acclaim for its accomplishments.) But the country whose program generates the most intense emotions — simultaneous envy and fear — is the Soviet Union. The reason, of course, is that the adversary relationship between the United States and the U.S.S.R. raises the importance of civil defense beyond the realm of mere technical accomplishment. According to civil defense advocates, the excellence of Soviet civil defense not only safeguards Russians, but also threatens Americans. Civil defense alters the stategic balance as much as weapons themselves do. If the Soviet Union builds and maintains an effective civil defense program, thereby making the survival of its citizens more likely, this might tempt Soviet leaders to attack the relatively unprotected United States. The concept of Mutually Assured Destruction (say the civil defense advocates) is dangerously flawed: destruction might not prove mutual.

Few people who have studied Soviet civil defense would argue that the program is not extensive. Even American governmental officials and private citizens who oppose civil defense programs in this country concede that the Soviet Union possesses the most elaborate planning in the world. But what this means is a subject of continual controversy. Is Soviet civil defense a mere "paper program"? To the degree that officials and citizens have carried it out, is it necessarily effective? And if it is effective, will it therefore tempt the Soviet leaders to think of nuclear war as worth the price their country would pay — civil defense or no?

One of the few available U.S. Government documents on this subject is a State Department Special Report entitled: *Soviet Civil Defense*. Released by the Director of Central Intelligence in July of 1978, the report outlines information about civil defense programs in the Soviet Union and draws conclusions to the degree its authors' considered possible. (Or permissible — it is uncertain how much relevant data remains classified.) Much of this report is general and uncontroversial. "Civil defense in the Soviet Union," it begins, "is an ongoing nationwide program under military control. The Soviets' strategic writings integrate civil defense into their military strategy. It is part of a general scheme of the likely origins, course, and consequences of a nuclear war." The report continues, indicating the basic concerns of the Soviet program. The abilities to protect people, to protect the sources of economic productivity, and to sustain the surviving population after an attack are the chief goals; for the most part, detailed plans to achieve these goals exist on paper.

However, most of the practical aspects of Soviet civil defense seem more difficult to assess. *Soviet Civil Defense* states that, "The Soviets probably have sufficient blast-shelter space in hardened command posts for virtually all the leadership elements at all levels (about 110,000 people)," but notes as well that "All fixed leaderships shelters...are vulnerable to direct attack..." Similarly, "Shelters at key economic installations could accomodate 12 to 24 percent of the total work force," but "Soviet plans do not call for sheltering the entire work force." Shelters for the urban population could accomodate 15 to 30 percent" by 1985; howver, "The critical decision to be made by the Soviet leaders in terms of sparing the population would be whether or not to evacuate cities." The report adds that "Only by evacuating the bulk of the urban population could they hope to achieve a marked reduction in the number of urban casualties." *Soviet Civil Defense* concludes by stating that "the Soviets" cannot have confidence...in the degree of protection their civil defense could afford them, given the many uncertainties attendant to a nuclear exchange."

This conclusion differs strongly from those which various interpreters of the document attribute to it. As Congressman Les Aspin of Wisconsin notes, "Most mass media summaries of the study have substantially distorted its contents." Those accounts mention the estimated Soviet expenditures on civil defense (two billion dollars per year) without acknowledging that the figure came "not from an exchange-rate calculation, but from how much it would cost the United States to duplicate the same program." Likewise, many accounts fail to indicate other issues discussed in *Soviet Civil Defense*: Soviet citizens' apathy toward civil defense; lack of evacuation rehearsals; ineffective plans for dispersing and protecting industry; and inadequate transportation. Representative Aspin argues that the largely ignored theme of this report is that "Soviet civil defense could not decisively affect the strategic balance" (*The Bulletin of the Atomic Scientists*, February, 1979). In short, some advocates of civil defense in the United States have quoted *Soviet Civil Defense* to reach a conclusion vastly different from what the document itself does.

Other writers and theoreticians have based their opinions on additional sources of information. One of the most outspoken is Leon Goure, the Director of the *Center of Soviet Studies* at a private research firm in Washington called Science Application, Incorporated. Goure has published widely on what he considers to be the Soviet civil defense threat. He writes that "Soviet spokesmen have consistently rejected the concept of equal security based on a U.S.-Soviet deterrence balance of 'mutual assured destruction.' " Instead, Goure asserts, the Soviets have undertaken preparations to increase the chances that the U.S.S.R. might survive and recover from a nuclear war; and he quotes Soviet spokesman G. Arbatov to this effect: "No country can set itself the aim of defeating the enemy at the cost of its own destruction" (American editor's comment, *Civil Defense: A Soviet View*, U.S. Government Printing Office, 1977).

Goure also claims that "the war-survival program being implemented by Soviet Civil Defense is considerably broader in scope than what is usually understood by civil defense in the West." Outlining its objectives, he writes, "It is by no means a mere paper program. It has been given the highest Party and Government endorsement, including by (Soviet President) Brezhnev personally, and is being implemented as a state law on a compulsory basis throughout the Soviet administrative and economic system..." Civil defense projects, according to Goure include classes in schools, construction of shelters, training of civil defense units, protection of industry and agriculture, and an urban evacuation plan. Goure concludes that "Given the Soviet view that a war-survival capability 'is becoming one of the most decisive strategic factors,' it appears that the civil defense program, along with the improvements in the capabilities of the Soviet Armed Forces, are intended to bring about a shift in the balance of forces in favor of the Soviet Union."

Other American commentators remain skeptical about these arguments. Fred M. Kaplan, for instance, who took part in the Arms Control Project at M.I.T.'s Center for International Studies during the late Seventies, has argued that too many observers exaggerate the significance of Soviet civil defense. Writing in *The Bulletin of the Atomic Scientists* (March, 1978), Kaplan states that according to such claims, "all but 2 to 10 percent of the Soviet population could be protected as well as a significant portion of its industrial base — so that full recovery could be assured in two to four years." He acknowledges that "If these reports are correct, the implications for arms control are dismaying." But he also argues that the basic analysis of many studies of Soviet civil defense "suffers from unrealistic assumptions, leaps of faith, violations of logic and a superficial understanding of the dynamics of a national economy. It appears from the available evidence that the Soviet civil defense program would be inadequate in the face of a large-scale nuclear attack." Most

of Kaplan's *Bulletin* article explains why seemingly frightful preparations are less significant than they appear.

Soviet programs, he says, "are neither effective nor strongly
emphasized." Training is poor; the populace is indifferent or even
contemptuous. (A standard Russian joke goes: "What do you do when
you hear the alert? "Put on a sheet and crawl to the cemetery —
slowly." "Why slowly?" "So you don't spread panic.") Soviet evacuation plans, though "impressive at first glance," are in fact "inadequate to protect anything close to 90 percent of the population."
Modes of transport include railroads and motor vehicles, but "Even
optimistic sources...take for granted that 20 percent of the urban population (17 million people) would have to walk." The   shelter
program, too, has major problems. Very few shelters have food stored
in them; only a few more have water. In addition, ventilation systems
are faulty or inadequate for the shelters they serve; blast shelters appear to be too weak to withstand the forces of an American nuclear attack; and expedient shelters — those supposedly designed to protect
tens of millions of ordinary citizens — are unrealistic considering
Russian weather during most of the year. Kaplan therefore asserts
that "only a small fraction of the population, whatever the season,
would be sheltered at all — and most of them, inadequately."

He argues instead that although the Soviet Union has, in fact,
undertaken a substantial civil defense project compared to the United
States, it serves other purposes than the bellicosity attributed to it by
Leon Goure and other observers. Noting that Soviet civil defense
dates back to the 1930s, Kaplan regards such programs as a long-time
concern of the party leadership. Civil defense also "helps maintain
order at home, being an excellent means both for reinforcing a
garrison-state mentality and for instilling a faith that the Communist
Party watches over and protects its people." Perhaps most important
of all is the residual fear of invasion — a reasonable fear, given the
Russian experience in both the First and Second World Wars. "In
sum," writes Kaplan, "...the patterns of Soviet history, the nature of
the Soviet political system, and the historically-rooted fear of invasion
among Soviet leaders suggest that the Soviet civil defense system...has
been and is seen by Soviet leaders as a hedge, as a defensive system"
(*The Bulletin of the Atomic Scientists*, April, 1978).

Consequently, the issue of Soviet civil defense ends up as controversial and as inconclusive as ever. Which position one takes may
depend more on political bias than on available data. Until American
observers obtain better information, their insights will remain uncertain.

What of American civil defense, meanwhile? Is it the shambles which so many critics consider it? Does it provide *any* defense for Americans in the event of nuclear attack? Is such a defense even possible? If so, and if not yet attained, should the U.S. government strive to achieve it? How? At what cost?

According to Federal Emergency Management Agency (FEMA) officials, the basic civil defense plan in the United States still emphasizes what they call "in-place community shelter." This involves identifying both public and private buildings — schools, town halls, auditoriums, hospitals, and so forth — and urging citizens to seek refuge in these places during a nuclear attack. Buildings marked with the yellow and purple radiation symbol are part of this system. In addition, FEMA planners intend to revive the now-defunct school civil defense system. This is the "duck and cover" system well-known to school children from the Fifties till the mid-Seventies.

FEMA publishes and distributes various sorts of literature to inform citizens of these plans. Booklets include *Protection in the Nuclear Age* and *In Time of Emergency*, both providing overviews of nuclear dangers and ways of dealing with them; a set of maps called "High Risk Areas" shows potential target areas throughout the United States. These publications and other (often more informal) sources of information allow any citizen to learn at least the rudiments of nuclear preparedness. Even FEMA officials admit that booklets of these types are only a start. However, few citizens express much interest in them anyway — although requests appear to be increasing lately — and the likelihood of successfully distributing more elaborate instructions is small. FEMA therefore stresses basic data on "Understanding the Hazards of Nuclear Attack," "Fallout Shelters, Public and Private," and "Improvising Fallout Protection."

Another dimension of American civil defense plans, however, has expanded more recently, and it is this which generates the most intense controversy. In 1978, President Carter signed PD41, a directive which reorganized U.S. civil defense and instituted (among other things) the Crisis Relocation Plan. This plan — generally called CRP — has drawn heavy fire from the start. (Its detractors sometimes ignore the usual acronym and simply call it CRAP.) Some critics fault CRP for doing too little too late. Others regard it as excessive — a dangerous overreaction. Still others like the general idea, but consider this specific plan a blueprint for pandemonium.

CRP involves evacuating high-risk communities within some 3,529 local jurisdictions and moving the populace to less dangerous areas. Citizens would leave their homes in time of crisis, would stay in host communities until the aftermath of an attack, and would then presumably return to their place of origin. Plans vary according to the needs of each community. For the most part, these involve people driving from cities to towns and rural areas, then setting up expedient fallout shelters under the supervision of local authorities. CRP does not provide for the stocking of food, water, and other emergency supplies in advance; the plan assumes that evacuees will bring stocks of some sort with them. Even FEMA officials concede that the arrangement is less than ideal. The government document entitled *U.S. Crisis Relocation* (February, 1981) asserts, however, that "This program could enable survival of roughly 80% of the U.S. population in a heavy attack."

Most critics of CRP consider these claims to be unwarranted. Some argue that civil defense planning of any sort gives citizens a false sense of security, and may even increase the likelihood of nuclear war; other object to what they regard as serious flaws in CRP logistics. Among these critics are liberal legislators, governors, mayors, and other government officials who regard civil defense planning as misdirected. In addition, various professional organizations — most notably, the Boston-based Phyicians for Social Responsibility — have directed considerable energy toward dispelling what they regard as dangerous illusions about nuclear "preparedness." Howard H. Hiatt, M.D., Dean of the Harvard School of Public Health, sums up this position succinctly: "Prevention is our only resource...." he told a Symposium on the Medical Consequences of Nuclear Weapons and Nuclear War in November of 1980. "We must heed the inescapable lesson of contemporary medicine: where treatment of a given disease is ineffective or where costs are insupportable, attention must be given to prevention."

Noting the intricacies of FEMA's Crisis Relocation Plan, the Center for Defense Information considers the program unrealistic. "FEMA assumes that a nuclear war could occur only after a period of rising tensions. At least three days would be needed to evacuate some areas, though large cities would require at least a week. For FEMA, a nuclear war must not come toon soon nor too late or its plans will not work." In addition, the Center comments that "An attack during the evacuation could result in more deaths than if the population had remained in place," and that "If the evacuation were carried out and the attack did not come for several weeks, great strains would be put on limited resources." The Center sees CRP as based on all sorts of untested assumptions and even wishful thinking. "The smooth coordination of an evacuation will require a high degree of volunteerism and calm behavior." In the absense of such attitudes, however, "problems would result at every juncture: automobiles would breakdown (sic) or run out of gas; some traffic personnel would go with their families rather than direct traffic; and not all essential workers would stay on the job."

Even certain U.S. government agencies have expressed skepticism about the plan. The most striking statement along these lines is the Office of Technology Assessment study entitled *The Effects of Nuclear War* (U.S. Government Printing Office, 1979). Although noting that "Evacuation is conceptually simple: people move from high-risk to low-risk areas," the OTA study perceives many dangerous uncertainties in this option. Knowing how much time is available, whether people would obey an evacuation order, and what possible targets might receive nuclear strikes all influence the success or failure of the plan. The OTA study therefore concludes its section on evacuation by stating that:

> The success of evacuation in the United States would likely vary from region to region. Generally, evacuation requires little planning in sparsely populated areas. In some areas, especially the Midwest and South, evacuation is feasible but requires special planning because fallout from attacks on ICBMs might mean longer evacuation distances. Evacuation from the densely populated Boston-to-Washington and Sacramento-to-San Diego corridors, with their tens of millions of people and limited relocation areas, may prove impossible.

In the meantime, while government officials and defense analysts debate the pros and cons of crisis relocation, a growing number of individual citizens have decided that they dislike the general idea, the specific form it takes in FEMA plans, or both. Various communities have also refused to participate in the plan during recent years. Cambridge, Massachusettes, for example, voted to reject CRP, and the city council chose instead to send its citizens a pamphlet outlining the dangers of nuclear attack. In Houston, Texas, John Caswell (Assistant Director of the city's Civil Defense Department) stated that it was "not feasible to try to evacuate a city the size of Houston," and the Houston mayor and county judge then rejected the plan. Similarly, the communities of Greensboro, North Carolina; Boulder, Colorado; Little Rock, Arkansas; and others have all refused to participate in CRP. Marilyn Braun, Director of the Guilford County (North Carolina) Emergency Management Assistance Agency, expressed what many other critics appear to believe: "We have no protection..for this threat. The Civil Defense publications...fail to address municipal needs for protection against blast and fallout. They also lack an adequate recovery system (*PSR Newsletter*, Summer, 1982).

But officials within FEMA claim that a perception of general hostility toward the plan would be inaccurate. Russell Clanahan, Public Information Offer for FEMA in Washington, told me, "Some communities have refused to take part, but not many. If a community refuses, it's news; if a community goes along, then it's no news. The media reports the refusals, and a momentum is made to appear which isn't really there." According to Clanahan, "It's hard to tell about the total numbers (of people objecting to CRP), but there is some indication about specific communities. There are 3,529 local jurisdictions in which CRP is possible. Of these, there are four categories for their response. The first is made up of communities which have indicated that they want CRP. There are 2,160 of these. Then there are 940 which have stated orally, but not formally, that they want CRP. Another 416 have not been contacted yet, but this number is diminishing. Only twenty-five have indicated they do not want to participate."

About the situation in general — public response to civil defense — Clanahan said,"The polls indicated that a majority of people in this country want some sort of civil defense. There's some skepticism about how much people can do regarding a nuclear war, but people want the government to do whatever can be done about it. The public attitude is basically that the public supports civil defense but feels that it wouldn't work perfectly. We agree. We aren't happy with the situation; we know what we're doing isn't ideal. But since we can't do everything, we've decided on CRP. You could save tens of millions of lives at a relatively small investment."

FEMA officials are also quick to defend their programs against specific criticisms. Frank J. Mollner, Chief of Emergency Management for Region VIII, explained some of the CRP policies to me, and he suggested that they are often misrepresented in the mass media. "The official position," said Mollner, "is that we will not force people to leave their community against their will. We will not force people to go to an area preassigned to them. What we want to urge is that they don't go from one high-risk area to another high-risk area. But there are some other aspects to this. One is that we know that some sixteen percent aren't going to go anyplace at all. Also, some people will get up and leave anyway even if you don't warn them. So there's more frustration to be gained by specifying locations for people."

When I asked him to demonstrate how CRP might work in a particular location, he drew some diagrams of the Denver area and indicated evacuations routes into the mountains. " This northwest part of the city is designed for evacuation west on Interstate-70. People aren't preassigned areas, but there is a flow of traffic into a number of different mountain communities. Part of the plan is to set up traffic control stations at the evacuation sites, so there would be someone counting off the number of cars coming through. Since Idaho Springs, for instance, can accommodate and estimated 35,000 refugees, the traffic control station can make sure that the number isn't exceeded."

I asked Mollner what would happen if someone insisted on entering Idaho Springs despite the traffic control station's insistence that he shouldn't. Mollner said, "If he insisted, then nobody could really stop him. At this point we're not set up to stop anyone." Then he added, "But there are all the other communities down the line — Granby, Glenwood Springs, and so forth — so it wouldn't matter if you got turned away at Idaho Springs. People won't feel badly about being turned away." Was he really so sure? When I asked him about the possibility of panic, Mollner discounted the risk. "Criticism about traffic jams and such ignores the reality of the situation. A Denver traffic jam doesn't last more than two hours. As to the comment that 'What if a car breaks down?' — I think it was that guy who writes for the *Rocky Mountain News* — that was an asinine remark. People would do what they always do: they would find some way of going around whatever was in the way. Keep in mind that we're assuming a seventy-two hour warning. At a rate of 1,000 cars per hour per lane — which is the design criterion for Colorado highways — it would actually be possible to evacuate target areas in Colorado within twenty-eight hours."

He mentioned, too, that with the current plans, "The warning time would allow the president to notify the governors before making a specific announcement to the public; and this would allow time to alert the Highway Patrol about the evacuation. Remember, the social scientists say that half the population won't believe the president or the governor anyway. People don't trust them. People look to their peers for a reaction. We're expecting a slow-building process. What we'll really see is that people get out more slowly; the crush will occur on the return to the target areas." But Mollner adds his own note of doubt to the otherwise confident claims: "There's a piece of this plan which makes sense, but I'm not sure if it's going to work. There's a time of free movement initially — people going wherever they want. This lasts about two hours. Afterwards, there's directed traffic. What we don't know is whether people will go along with that."

In fact, nobody knows if anybody will go along with *any* of CRP. FEMA officials maintain that the plan is workable, and that — whatever else — it's better than nothing. But CRP remains unpersuasive to many Americans. Most survivalists are even more skeptical. Doubts concerning the government's sincerity and competence therefore become not only a source of frustration and rage, but also an impetus to seek some sort of alternative. For many people, the alternative is obvious: survivalism.

Some survivalists (including many of the most active) see their private efforts towards nuclear preparedness as a reluctant second choice to what they might actually have undertaken. FEMA's programs, in their view, are problematic not for being too much, but for being far too little. They do not see survivalism and civil defense as antithetical. Survivalism is simply the escape hatch. The United States is weak and vulnerable, they say; in place of agencies and plans designed to protect citizens, this country has come to rely on ineffectual paper programs. The resulting dilemma prompts them to suggest drastic solutions.

The writers of *The Nuclear War Survival Bulletin*, claim that "If the country is going to survive we must stop thinking of tiny government appropriations. We cannot have annual CD expeditures rise from $120 million to $500 million over ten years...it will be too little too late." Instead, this conservative group (based in Coos Bay, Oregon) recommends massive programs. "We must get our annual expenditures up to the *$10 billion* level (their emphasis), and keep them there for at least ten years." The NWS Research Bureau suggests a comprehensive civil defense program stressing education, equipment, shelter, and food storage. In addition, the group urges the American government to undertake four additional projects: 1) a Civil Defense

Command organized within the military; 2) removal of all land-based missiles in the United States; 3) construction of an anti-ballistic missile system; 4) construction of high-technology "directed energy defense," such as lasers and particle-beam weapons (*The Nuclear War Survival Bulletin*, March 1981).

As if recognizing that even conservative politicians will balk at trying to implement these measures, the NWS Research Bureau suggests an alternative. *"The time for casual preparations is over; serious survival planning is called for* (their emphasis)....the prudent family will set the goal of accumulating all the items which will allow self-sufficient living for *at least* one year." This group, in short, advocates suvivalism as a necessary response to what its writers regard as inadequate civil defense. Recommendations follow the standard survivalist agenda: move out of high risk areas; build a shelter; store food and water. The benefits, they say, will be more than just the material ones. "Once you start this you will find a sense of calm and independence which is often lacking in the modern American lifestyle," writes the author of The Nuclear War Suvival Bulletin (March, 1982). "A small minority recognize (sic) the danger and make (sic) the adjustments which assure their families (sic) survival...no matter what the government does...or does not do (elisions in original)."

Another influential spokesperson is Leon Goure. Dr. Goure, quoted earlier regarding Soviet civil defense, recommends an increase in American efforts to offset this perceived threat. He is skeptical, however, about the American government's abilities to undertake a successful program. Some of his skepticism focuses on problems within the current civil defense bureaucracy. In a *Survive* magazine interview, Goure gave an example of the problem:

> Do you know the plan for the District of Columbia's evacuation? It assumes that part of the population will be evacuated to Virginia. O.K. But the plan in principle stops in the middle of the 14th Street Bridge. We don't know what they will do there because Virginia won't coordinate with them. The officials from D.C. were prohibited from doing a survey in the Virginia territory. You see, the Federal Civil Defense Act of 1950 as amended states that this is a voluntary association. Each state may observe its borders and refuse to cooperate.

Goure therefore advocates that citizens undertake individual programs to increase their chances of survival. "I do not believe the

government will take care of all your problems," he told Will
Brownell (*Survive*, May/June, 1982). "People should have this information (regarding shelters and survival planning). And the shelter
doesn't have to be fancy to be effective; you don't have to spend
$30,000 for a shelter. Most people can manage with a protected
basement." Goure also recommends storing food, water, extra
clothing, ventilation and sanitation equipment, first-aid supplies,
tools, "and other items too numerous to mention." Whether by this
name, by another, or by none at all, Goure is recommending survivalism.

Such recommendations bolster the already strong survivalist in-
clination to go it alone. The government will fritter away everyone's
time and money; individuals can do the job much better. This, in any
case, is the common opinion within the survival movement. Ironically, some civil defense officials wouldn't object to survivalists' private
efforts. Survivalists often see FEMA as the enemy — or at least as
"the ultimate 'turkey farm'...this moribund collection of in-
competents..." as *The Nuclear War Survival Bulletin* (March, 1981)
puts it — but FEMA officials do not necessarily hold survivalists in
equal contempt. Some even condone or praise survivalists for their efforts, since private preparation of this sort heightens public awareness
of the problems involved and takes at least a little pressure off the
government's responsibilities. Frank Mollner of FEMA's Region VIII,
for instance, told me that he has only specific reservations about the
survival movement. "With the exception of their shielding
themselves from the rest of the community — fine. Their information
is good. Their technology is good. But this must be an effort of the
community working together. The scary idea is putting aside your
own food and water and then protecting it."

Russell Clanahan, Public Affairs Officer for FEMA in
Washington, provided a more detailed opinion. "If you've studied the
movement," he told me, "you know there are many kinds of survivalists. There's a fringe element — very into guns — and of course
we can't approve of that. But the great majority have read the
literature, have read what we've put out, and they realize that our
resources are limited. We can't do as much as we'd like. And so they
realize it's important to do what they can about shelters and so forth."
I asked him about the commercial survivalists — those who produce
food, equipment, and services for sale. "There could be charlatans, of
course," Clanahan responded, "but as long as people are selling what
they claim to sell, it's all right with us."

And so it continues: opinion and rebuttal, claim and counterclaim, reiteration and qualification. What is the concerned observer to make of it all? Is civil defense the alternative to survivalism? Is survivalism the alternative to civil defense? Are these forms of preparation equally useful in solving the nuclear dilemma? Counterproductive? Dangerous?

In order to gain a better sense of the issues involved, it's worthwhile to examine the special characteristics of civil defense and survivalism, their advantages, their disadvantages. This may allow some perspective on what degree of safety each orientation provides against the risk of nuclear war.

Civil defense, according to the current Department of Defense definition, comprises

> *All those activities and measures designed or undertaken to:* **a.** minimize the effects upon the civilian population caused or which would be caused by an enemy attack upon the United States; **b.** deal with the immediate emergency conditions which would be created by any such attack; and **c.** effectuate emergency repairs to, or the emergency restoration of, vital utilities and facilities destroyed by any such attack (from *The Defense Monitor*, **XI**, No. 5, 1982).

This definition — implicitly if not explicitly — reveals the nature of civil defense in this country. It is dependent on formal policy. As such, it remains subject to the vagaries of bureaucratic function. Its chief advantage lies in being relatively equitable. Civil defense serves the public in general, not just those citizens who can afford it. Its disadvantages are expense, red tape, and possible adverse effects on geopolitical stability.

In contrast, survivalism is private endeavor to establish or increase personal security in the face of potential disasters. Survivalism depends entirely on the impetus of individuals, families, or other independent groups. Its main advantage stems precisely from this independence: survivalists can implement plans according to their own preferences, finances, and levels of commitment. The disadvantage is a side effect of precisely such advantages. Because survivalists go about their preparations while people around them do not, their activities tend to be isolating — at least for the survivalists.

Civil defense and survivalism could theoretically function side by side. Just as modern transportation involves the use of both mass transit and private vehicles, so almost might nuclear preparedness employ public and individual preparations at the same time. This arrangement already exists to some degree. What complicates the situation is that the risk of nuclear war raises the stakes to the level of life and death; and many Americans (whether rightly or not) consider current civil defense programs to be almost lethally inadequate. This is turn makes survivalism even more controversial. Although survivalists themselves protest that they are not a privileged few buying their way to safety, the fact remains that many persons who might wish to plan for emergencies simply cannot afford the expense. Nuclear preparedness, like quality health care, lies beyond most Americans' budgets.

Something worth noting is that in the countries most vulnerable to nuclear attack, extensive civil defense and survivalism seem to be mutually exclusive more often than not. Sweden, Norway, Switzerland, the Soviet Union, and China all stress the importance of civil defense, but there is little or no survivalist activity visible among their citizens. Of course, the Soviet and Chinese governments would be likely to discourage such individual preparation anyway — if, in fact, the leaders of these nations allow it at all. But Sweden, Norway, and Switzerland are another matter. Nothing to date indicates the presence of survivalists in these countries. By contrast, the United States and Great Britain — both nations with relatively weak civil defense programs — show signs of burgeoning survivalism. The trend is more pronounced in the United States. Britain, however, seems to be developing quickly in this regard. *Protect and Survive Monthly* is already a popular counterpart to the American *Survive* magazine; various companies have gone into business selling shelters; and Fishergate Hill, Lancashire, boasts England's first "nuclear survival equipment centre." There are some heavily targeted western nations, meanwhile, which lack both civil defense and survivalist activity: France and West Germany are two prominent examples. But generally speaking, the pattern holds true that survivalism develops only where the inhabitants of a country feel that their government has neglected to provide for civil defense.

Of itself, the presence or absence of civil defense or survivalism does little to address the most crucial issues about them, however. Do they make nuclear war less likely? More so? And in the event of a war, would either be effective in protecting people from its consequences?

The question of greater or lesser likelihood reveals the house of cards which makes up current theory on nuclear deterrence. Nigel Calder's book *Nuclear Nightmares* explains the peculiar logic involved here.

> The abiding image in Western deterrence theory is of American H-bombs exploding over Moscow and killing most of the inhabitants. Soviet leaders, knowing that this can happen, are thereby deterred from any nuclear adventure. Conversely, the Americans appreciate them. This state of affairs is known as "mutually assured destruction"(appropriately, MAD for short)

The problem with civil defense within this context is that any substantial preparations may decrease rather than increase relative security. "The population is protected by deterrence and the idea of mutual deterrence depends on the population being vulnerable," Calder explains. "It is not playing fair, in the game of 'mutually assured destruction,' to try to minimize the effects of the other fellows' strike. Indeed, if you start building strong shelters and drawing up plans for evacuating your cities, you could upset the balance of terror." Calder goes on to say that "Your actions imply, at best, that you do not have unlimited faith in deterrence; at worst it means that you are trying to avoid 'assured destruction' on your side in order to be able to fight and win a nuclear war." These assumptions give rise to the widespread worries about Soviet civil defense. For much of the same reasons, they foster concern about the possible effects of American civil defense programs.

FEMA officials and other advocates of civil defense argue that nuclear preparedness does not necessarily increase the risk of war. "The view is sometimes expressed that providing some protection for our people would make a war more likely," states a booklet entitled *Questions* published by FEMA's Region VIII. "This is nonsense. It's like saying that putting lifeboats on an ocean liner will lead the ship's captain to seek out confrontations with icebergs." This booklet goes on to quote President Truman on the subject:

> Everyone in this country must face the fact that civil defense is, and will continue to be just as vital to American security as our Armed Forces, our defense production, and our aid to allies and friends abroad (sic). Civil defense is another indispensable part of our total security program. I really believe that anyone who

reflects upon this matter will understand why that is so. Every weakness in civil defense increases an aggressor's temptation to attack us. Every weakness in our civil defense adds to the strength of a potential enemy....

But clever analogies and thirty-year-old policy statements do not really clarify the many issues involved here. Nuclear weapons and strategies are much more complex today than they were when President Truman issued his statement in 1952, and civil defense serves more than merely a lifeboat function.

Admiral Gene LaRocque's Center for Defense Information argues in a recent issue of *The Defense Monitor* (**XI** No. 5, 1982) that civil defense programs currently considered by the administration do, in fact, increase the risk of nuclear war. "Effective protection and national survival in a nuclear war, with today's vast number of nuclear weapons and their destructive power, are impossible. The active pursuit of and belief in a civil defense program of significant size will increase the likelihood of nuclear war." The reasons, according to *The Defense Monitor* consultants, are that "the pressure to demonstrate resolve by preparing for evacuation and leadership dispersal...will grow (during a crisis). Either side's decision to evacuate the cities could trigger the nuclear war it was designed to prevent." Civil defense in its current form is "an effort to manipulate and mobilize the American public by diverting attention from the real problem, the dangerous and dynamic nature of the arms race."

For these reasons, survivalism may be less destablizing than civil defense — at least on a global scale — and to this extent, may be preferable to national programs. Instability within the United States is another matter. Many people regard survivalists as "kooks" preoccupied with catastrophe; on the other hand, some people may find themselves alarmed by the sight of fellow-passengers (to extend FEMA's metaphor) abandoning ship. Survivalists argue that they can prepare in whatever way they want. For the most part, this argument is correct. And the consequences of their activities may prove less worrisome, all in all, than a governmental-sponsored civil defense buildup and its possible consequences.

But these considerations leave the most crucial questions still unanswered. Could civil defense programs help people survive a nuclear war? Could survivalist preparations? Is it even *possible* to survive a nuclear war?

This is the crux of the matter.

Chapter Seven

But How Can Anyone Survive?

In the short time since its publication, Jonathan Schell's *The Fate of the Earth* has become a kind of shibboleth within the United States. Anti-nuclear activists praise the book for its eloquence and its depth of insight; advocates of American nuclear pre-eminence attack it as simplistic and inaccurate. Schell's work has been called everything from "a Bible for the nuclear age" to "one of the worst (books) ever printed on nuclear war." Nobody seems to have a mild opinion of it. No doubt the controversy will continue for a long time. Yet whatever its limitations or merits, *The Fate of the Earth* has unquestionably intensified the nuclear debate in this country.

It's a complex, difficult, emotional debate. Disarmament is only one of its controversial aspects — though perhaps the most conspicuous. Other issues include military strategy, the dynamics of nuclear proliferation, the task of assessing hostile nations' goals, and the ethics of war. To make matters worse, all of these issues intertwine with each other into a seemingly hopeless knot. And of course the issues are anything but academic.

The scope of a book about survivalism precludes analysis of the nuclear debate in all the necessary detail. The issues are relevant, and some of them — such as the sporadic pace of U.S.-Soviet arms control talks — have spurred many Americans' survival preparations. Unfortunately, these issues remain beyond the reach of the present inquiry.

There is a fundamental exception, however: simply the question of survival itself. Can anyone survive a nuclear war? Would it extinguish all life on earth? Would it wipe out humanity? And if not, who would survive? Would the survivalists survive?

The controversy over *The Fate of the Earth* gives an indication of how little agreement exists when people try to answer these questions. Jonathan Schell's thesis is that given the various possible consequences of nuclear war — radiation, climatic changes, ecological damage, disease, and so forth — "a full-scale nuclear holocaust could lead to the extinction of mankind." Contrary to what some of his critics have claimed, Schell is actually rather circumspect about the likelihood of extinction, and never states that it would be inevitable. "To say that human extinction is a certainty would, of course, be a misrepresentation — just as it would be a misrepresentation to say that extinction can be ruled out," he writes in *The Fate of the Earth*. But though "We are left with uncertainty, and are forced to make our decisions in a state of uncertainty," Schell stresses the possibility that human extinction *might* result from a full-scale nuclear war.

In contrast, other observers, including survivalists, take issue with even these tentative conclusions. Will Brownell, for instance, writing in the September/October, 1982, issue of *Survive* magazine, attacks Schell for the various technical errors in his book. He then states that "Many of these (errors) you've probably heard before from the Doomies, such as the myth that nearly everyone will get cancer after a nuclear war.... Unfortunately, Schell has merely perpetuated many of the unsubstantiated nuclear myths so popular in Doomie circles." Other survivalist writers respond less to Schell's book than to the widespread belief that nuclear war will destroy the human race. This was certainly part of what prompted Bruce Clayton to write *Life After Doomsday*. "There is no need to lie to people about the effects of a nuclear war," he states in his introduction. "The truth is bad enough. The damage done by making the threat seem worse than it really is cannot be easily dispelled. The exaggerated tales of total annihilation convince people that survival is impossible. This is not true."

Survivalist writers sometimes make valid points in this regard. Many Americans do, in fact, assume outright that surviving a nuclear war would be impossible, and they often base their assumption on limited or faulty data. Survivalists like Bruce Clayton have performed a valuable service in drawing attention to inaccuracies in books about nuclear war and its consequences. Certainly the nuclear debate is important partly as a means of clarifying issues which many people have ignored or distorted. Inaccurate information serves nobody's best interests. Neither do half-hearted attempts at interpretation or speculation. But contrary to what some persons imply, anti-nuclear writers and activitists do not have a monoply on limited data or specious reasoning. Survivalists, too, run the risk of twisting the truth. In the course of interviewing survivalists, I've heard statements which show little connection with available information about nuclear war, and I've heard predictions which reveal more than a healthy dose of wishful thinking. One man, for instance, told me that survival would be "no sweat. Nuclear war wouldn't have much effect on my plans. The dangers have been exaggerated." Also, a young woman explained that "Fallout really isn't a problem. If some falls on you, just brush it off." And too many others imply that the aftermath of a nuclear war would certainly be difficult, but also challenging — even exciting at times — something to test one's mettle, like a long camping trip. Then there are the extreme opinions, such as Kurt Saxon's: "a nuclear holocaust will be a blessing for the survivors."

Precisely because the possibility of nuclear war evokes intense emotions — bewilderment, dread, anger, and sometimes a strange kind of longing — the issues involved challenge everyone's ability to perceive them clearly. There is a constant temptation to oversimplify the situation. Nuclear war is no big deal. Nuclear war is the utter end-all. All or nothing. Either/or. And the risk is therefore that dealing with the possibility grows more difficult, not easier, and more dangerous, not less so.

Many books deal with the effects of nuclear weapons, but relatively few examine the possible consequences of nuclear warfare. The distinction is important. Hundreds of tests — the detonations of atomic and hydrogen bombs under controlled circumstances — have provided much data regarding how nuclear weapons work and how they affect their surroundings. Extrapolation has revealed still more about these phenomena. In addition, certain events, such as the irradiation of American soldiers on maneuvers during the 1950s, have allowed a glimpse of what nuclear explosions do even when people are in "safe" areas. But little information exists about nuclear war as such. The exception is, of course, the bombing of Hiroshima and Nagasaki at the end of the Second World War — hardly a trivial exception — and yet the scale of that disaster compared to what the world faces today makes any sort of prediction based on it almost absurd.

Various studies, however, allow at least for some degree of conjecture. Samuel Glasstone and Philip J. Dolan's *The Effects of Nuclear Weapons* is the basic technical handbook on the subject — a compendium of data on blast, thermal radiation, nuclear radiation, electromagnetic pulse, biological effects, and other consequences of nuclear weapons. Other studies examine the effects of multiple detonations. For instance, the National Academy of Sciences undertook a study to estimate the environmental and ecological impact of a nuclear war, and in 1975 published its report, *Long-Term Worldwide Effects of Multiple Nuclear-Weapons Detonations*. This report examines possible effects on "the atmosphere and climate, natural terrestrial ecosystems, agriculture and animal husbandry, the aquatic environment, and both sometic and genetic effects upon humans." More recently, two extensive reports have focused on how nuclear attacks affect human populations. One is *Hiroshima and Nagasaki: The Physical, Medical, and Social Effects of the Atomic Bombings*, which summarizes current data on the events. The other is a U.S. Office of Technology Assessment study entitled *The Effects of Nuclear War*, which undertakes "to describe the effects of a nuclear war on the civilian populations, economies, and societies of the United States and the Soviet Union." There are, in addition, numerous more specific studies which explore individual aspects of a nuclear war. Collectively, these sources make it possible to gain at least an overview of what a war might mean to individuals and society.

What follows is not a comprehensive examination of the subject. Rather, it is a summary of the basic issues involved and how they apply to the survivalist agenda. The simplest way to proceed is by considering each of these issues separately at first, then together. A final discussion focuses on whether current data supports the survivalists' assumptions that they could, in fact, survive a nuclear war.

Blast

One of the problems (at least for laypersons) in trying to understand the effects of nuclear weapons is how to make technical language come alive. Information is indispensable, but what does it *mean?* Glasstone in *The Effects of Nuclear Weapons* writes that "Many structures will suffer some damage from air blast when the overpressure in the blast wave, i.e., the excess over the atmospheric pressure (14.7 pounds per square inch at standard sea level conditions), is about one-half pound per square inch or more." Agreed. And yet most people without appreciable scientific background will finish that sentence knowing almost as little as they did before starting it. Likewise, learning that a one-megaton bomb exploded in the air produces an overpressure of five pouunds per square inch (psi) — this according to the OTA's study — does not help our understanding. Fortunately for non-scientists, some of the information about nuclear weapons can be considerably more graphic. The OTA study notes, for instance, that a five psi overpressure "will exert a force of more than 180 tons on the wall of a typical two-story house." But what brings the issue home for most people is what they see for themselves. Photos: mangled utility poles; flipped-over trucks; a house reduced to rubble.

Most survivalist writers seem straightforward about the danger of a nuclear blast. Bruce Clayton includes a discussion in *Life After Doomsday* which covers the most pertinent basic data. "Probably the most difficult thing to grasp about the blast wave is that it is actually composed of two effects which happen at once," he explains, and then elaborates mostly on information acquired from Glasstone's book about overpressure, dynamic pressure, and their effects on people and buildings. Other theoreticians, such as Cresson Kearny, provide much shorter discussions. Most of Kearny's remarks concern the use of improvised shelters to protect people from blast. Duncan Long also touches on these matters but even more briefly: his comments in *Nuclear War Survival* take up a single paragraph. Survivalist treatments of this subject generally stress the need to avoid being near target zones in the first place. Kearny notes that "Most Americans would greatly improve their chances of surviving a nuclear attack if they were to evacuate probable target areas before an attack or make or improve fallout shelters in dispersed locations..." Clayton, too, emphasizes the advantages of evacuation, although he notes that '- 'You *could* be hit by a structure-damaging shock wave even in the most remote parts of the country."

For the most part, survivalists' decisions to relocate away from target areas provide them with as much relative safety from nuclear blast as obtainable. Those who fail to relocate in time would obviously suffer the same consequences as non-survivalists. In addition, it is possible that some nuclear warheads might miss their targets and explode in supposedly safe areas. Yet survivalists' remote locations give

them a substantial margin of safety. The phenomenon of nuclear blast
— being short-lived and relatively localized — is the effect of nuclear
weapons which survivalists could most consistently avoid.

Heat

Heat presents a more complex danger to survivalists. One of the
results of a nuclear detonation is the release of enormous quantities of
thermal radiation. Weapons generate temperatures "estimated to be
several tens of million degrees," according to Glasstone; and though
the damage resulting from thermal radiation depends on various factors (among them total yield of the bomb, height of burst, distance of
objects from the burst point, and the state of the atmosphere), heat is
usually one of the most destructive effects of a nuclear weapon.

The basic sources of information on this subject are blunt about
the consequences. The three direct consequences of thermal radiation
on humans are flashblindness, retinal burns, and skin/flesh burns.
Flashblindness, according to the OTA study, "can last for several
minutes, after which recovery is total." A one-megaton explosion
could cause flashblindness at distances of up to thirteen miles on a
clear day or 53 miles on a clear night. As for retinal burns, these result
from the lens of the eye focusing the flash onto the retina. The OTA
study notes that "At Hiroshima and Nagasaki, there were many cases
of flashblindness, but only one case of retinal burn, among the survivors." Skin burns result from higher intensities of light than those
which would generate flashblindness or retinal burns alone. According to the OTA study, a one-megaton explosion "can cause first-
degree burns...at distances of about 7 miles," "second-degree burns..
.at distances of about 6 miles," and "third-degree burns...at distances
of up to 5 miles..." Glasstone presents similar data in *The Effects of
Nuclear Weapons*, but goes into considerably more detail about the
consequences. The implications are frightening: "20 to 30 percent of
the fatal casualties in Hiroshima and Nagasaki were caused by flash
burns."

In addition to the direct effects of thermal radiation —
flashblindness, retinal burns, and skin burns — the heat resulting
from nuclear explosions can produce some indirect effects as well.
Glasstone notes that "The indirect (or secondary) burns are referred
to as 'contact burns' or 'flame burns'" — those resulting from fires
which thermal radiation may ignite. The OTA study is more graphic in
its description. Beds, furniture, and entire houses may ignite in the

aftermath of a nuclear explosion. Non-thermal damage "to water heaters, furnaces, electrical circuits, or gas lines would ignite fires where fuel is plentiful." The overall result might exceed the damage from individual fires alone: "It is possible that individual fires, whether caused by thermal radiation or by blast damage to utilities, furnaces, etc., would coalesce into a mass fire that would consume all structures over a large area."

Survivalist writers acknowledge most of this information. Burce Clayton's discussion in *Life After Doomsday* is again the most comprehensive, and renders technical data relatively intelligible. Clayton even considers aspects of the problem which other survivalists ignore. He notes, for instance, that nuclear weapons might spread fires beyond the zone of initial destruction. There is also the possibility of forest fires. "A wildfire can cover ground quickly," he writes, "traveling as fast as ten miles an hour in some cases. Even if you select a retreat site that will escape all nuclear weapons effects, you will still have to give some thought to the delayed arrival of forest fires." Yet despite these and other signs that survivalists recognize the possibilities of fires after a nuclear war, few seem to see the implications. It is not simply a question of "ordinary" forest fires, no matter how deadly. A recent article in the Swedish journal *Ambio* (11: 2-3, 1982), for instance, notes that "As a result of a nuclear war vast areas of forests will go up in smoke — corresponding at least to the combined land mass of Denmark, Norway and Sweden." In addition, tremendous fires "will burn for weeks in cities and industrial centers," and 'fires will also rage across croplands...'

The result of such conflagrations would exceed the more localized effects which survivalists anticipate from thermal radiation. Survivalists might, in fact, escape the most immediate consequences of weapons-induced heat. But the drastic side effects are another matter. The consequences actually go far beyond those which most people acknowledge. Since these consequences involve another aspect of nuclear war — that of atmospheric damage — a separate section of this chapter will examine it shortly.

Fallout

Fallout is, of course, one of the most intensely dreaded effects of nuclear weapons. Even survivors of blast and heat from a nuclear attack might succumb to the consequences of fallout; moreover, fallout endangers not only those persons in the immediate vicinity of a detonation, but also people in more distant areas. "Local" fallout from a single bomb can affect hundreds of square miles. In addition, there is the risk from delayed fallout — particles which remain suspended in the atmosphere for weeks, months, or even longer, settling to earth far from the detonation site. These various phenomena, when considered separately or together, justifiably alarm people who might have to deal with them.

Various survivalist writers object to what they consider the common exaggerations of the danger. Popular writers and anti-nuclear activists, they say, have distorted the facts and made an already bad situation even worse: consequently, most uninformed laypersons assume that fallout from a nuclear war guarantees the extinction of humanity. Some survivalists call this the *On the Beach* mentality — a reference to Nevil Shute's doomsday novel. Bruce Clayton, Cresson Kearny, and other theoreticians have responded by trying to dispell what they regard as nuclear myths concerning fallout. Kearny, for example, writes in *Nuclear War Survival Skills* of the common belief that "Fallout radiation from a nuclear war would poison the air and all parts of the environment," and derides the conclusion that "It would kill everyone." He analyzes current data on fallout, assesses the risks, and recommends measures (such as expedient shelters) to reduce the threat. "Those who hold exaggerated beliefs about the dangers from nuclear weapons," he states, "must first be convinced that nuclear war would not inevitably be the end of them and everything worthwhile." Similarly, Bruce Clayton criticizes what he calls "anti-nuke activists," and he attempts to set the record straight. His *Life After Doomsday* and two "Nuclear Nonsense" articles (*Survive*, Fall and Winter, 1981) cover much the same ground as in Kearny's book, though with different emphases. Clayton stresses that "the real danger it (fallout) represents is much less than the legendary danger." Nuclear doomsayers distort their data, he claims; "the myth that a nuclear war means a poisoned world for thousands of years is not true."

What *is* true, then? To answer this question, we should consider the information presented in current survivalist manuals, and examine its accuracy and completeness. (Bruce Clayton's *Life After Doomsday* goes into the most detail on these issues; for this reason, and because it is probably the most influential book among survivalists concerned about nuclear war, I have relied on it more than on others.)

Variables. Clayton conceded that "the amount of fallout formed and its distribution over the landscape depend on many interacting factors, such as the design of the weapon, the size of the particles, the height of the explosion above the ground, and weather conditions at the time." Kearny also mentions these variables. "Exceptions (to a two-week shelter period following a nuclear attack)," he notes, "would be in areas of extremely heavy fallout such as might occur downwind from important targets attacked with many weapons..." Other writers, such as C. Bruce Sibley, author of *Surviving Doomsday* also mention variables in calculating the effects of fallout.

Types of Fallout. Clayton, Kearny, Sibley, and most other survivalist writers distinguish between local and delayed fallout. Clayton goes into the most detail. "After a surface burst, the fallout gradually settles to the ground over a period of about twenty-four hours. This is the *local fallout*...," he writes. "After the first day, the particles remaining in the air are so fine that they take weeks or months to finally reach the ground, usually carried by drops of rain or flakes of snow. This is the *delayed fallout*" (his italics). Generally, survivalist theoreticians go into more detail about local fallout than about delayed fallout, since it is the kind which presents the most acute danger to survivors of a nuclear war.

Duration of radioactivity. Kearney's *Nuclear War Survival Skills* offers the most basic explanation of this issue. Kearney emphasizes that "the danger from fallout radiation lessens with time. The radioactive decay, as this lessening is called, is rapid at first, then gets slower and slower." Charts demonstrate his claims. Clayton's book explains by means of more elaborate examples. *Life After Doomsday* also considers ways of diminishing the effects of radiation differently from Kearny's. (Clayton stresses escaping areas of high-level radiation as well as reducing the effects of fallout by construction of shelters; Kearny stresses building basic, spur-of-the-moment shelters.) In addition, Clayton criticizes common assumptions about fallout more explicitly than others do: "Most fallout studies," he writes, "use 'worst case' assumptions which make the problem look much more serious than it really is."

Harmful effects. None of the survivalist manuals actually dismisses the potential for damage resulting from fallout. Clayton's book, for example, enumerates more dangers in this regard than most non-survivalist treatments of the same subject. Ecological effects of local fallout, internal radiation exposure, and effects of delayed fallout are all subjects which he treats at length. Generally speaking, he admits that the consequences of fallout radiation would be substantial risks to human health. He also described deleterious effects on animals and plants. However, Clayton qualifies these descriptions in such a way as to downplay some of the danger. "By simply avoiding contaminated food and water for a month or so after the attack," he writes when referring to the possibility of iodine-131 poisoning, "you can eliminate most of the risk." Of strontium-90 contamination, he states, "There *will* be locations too heavily contaminated to use for agriculture, but they will be limited in extent...Strontium-90 won't be that big a problem."

Clayton also attacks what he considers to be gross overstatements of related problems. Writing in *Survive* magazine (Fall, 1981), Clayton argues that "Some of the more pernicious myths are those which state that even if survival of the war itself were possible, the survivors would eventually be wiped out by radiation-induced cancers." One of his most consistent targets is Helen M. Caldicott, M.D., founder and president of the anti-nuclear organization called Physicians for Social Responsibility. In her book *Nuclear Madness*, Caldicott claims that "The long-term fallout effects in the countries bombed would give rise to other epidemics. Within five years, leukemia would be rampant. Within 15 to 20 years, solid cancers of the lung, breast, bowel, stomach, and thyroid would strike down survivors." Clayton's response is to counter with information about Japanese who survived the bombings of Hiroshima and Nagasaki.

> The predicted incidence of leukemia among adults who had been exposed to 100 to 200 rems of radiation would be *between two and four cases per thousand* former radiation patients. Surviving severely irradiated children who had been under 10 years old at the time of the war would be twice as susceptible, which means four to eight cases of leukemia per thousand. Now I admit that a leukemia rate approaching 1 percent of the radiation patients would be a terrible tragedy, but it wouldn't exactly mean the end of our species, would it? (italics in original)

Similarly, he argues that "over the period from 15 to 50 years following the war, the *heavily irradiated* survivors as a group would produce three cases of cancer where we would normally have expected to find only two" (italics in original). He goes on to write that "In Japan, out of 109,000 A-bomb survivors, only 5,700 were heavily irradiated. Of these, between 1960 and 1970 (15 to 24 years later) a total of 47 died of cancer, as opposed to an expected cancer death toll of 30." Clayton concludes that "Somehow that doesn't sound quite the same as being 'struck down' in wholesale lots."

Another frequent claim which Clayton dismisses as myth are those which concern genetic damage and mutation. As elsewhere, he quotes Dr. Caldicott's *Nuclear Madness:*

> Exposure of the reproductive organs to the immense quantities of radiation in the explosions would result in reproductive sterility in many. An increased incidence of spontaneous abortions and deformed offspring, and a massive increase in both dominant and recessive mutations, would also result. Rendered intensely radioactive, the planet Earth would eventually become inhabited by bands of roving humanoids — mutants barely recognizable as members of our species.

Clayton's response is to dismiss these claims almost out of hand. "If you look closely at that first passage you may discover, as I did, the paradoxical notion that sterile parents would give birth to roving bands of unrecognizable mutants through spontaneous abortions...but perhaps I am being too critical." He criticizes these assumptions in more detail. "As for spontaneous abortions," he writes, "it is important to realize that these unpleasant events are nature's way of *preventing* the birth of malformed infants. We should be thankful for them, not fearful of them." He continues to counter other aspects of Caldicott's argument; speaking of the Hiroshima and Nagasaki survivors, for instance, he states that studies of them (in the 1977 National Academy of Sciences report on nuclear war) "showed among other things that there was no abnormal incidence of genetic disease among the offspring of the irradiated survivors. Even that one extra malformed infant (predicted by the study) failed to put in an appearance."

Other writers seem as quick to downplay medical consequences of radiation exposure. For example, C. Bruce Sibley writes at some length about the uncertainties attendant in predicting biological side effects from fallout. "Some argue that there is a point where any increase in the radiation exposure level will threaten the long-term health of the individual," Sibley writes in *Surviving Doomsday*. "Other experts say that there is no threshold and that radiation can affect health at whatever level it might be. The author prefers to make

his case with mother Nature. Everybody living on this planet is subject to small amounts of Background Radiation (sic)..." Sibley then
extrapolates from this assumption: "The human race and the planet's
whole ecology evolved in this sea of background radiation for millions
of years. Doubtless nature had intended it to be just so because over
this vast passage of time she has caused subtle changes to occur in
new generations of the planet's living organisms." He does not quite
come to say Radiation Is Good for You — but he does come close.

How accurate is the survivalists' information on fallout? Surely
this depends on the survivalist in question. Data ranges from the
relatively thorough (such as Clayton's) to the cursory (such as
Sibley's), with most of it somewhere in between. Much of it does, in
fact, seem to be more detailed, and sometimes more heavily substan-
tiated, than that which many disarmament activists distribute. But is
it therefore adequate? Does it answer all the questions which it raises?
Or is it — despite an appearance of detail — actually more limited
than it appears?

To assess survivalists' technical data on radiation, I submitted
various articles and chapters of books to two physicists for review. I
also interviewed three other scientists in this regard. The two
physicists were Chris D. Zafiratos and Robert Ristinen, both professors at the University of Colorado at Boulder. Zafiratos considered the
material to be "basically correct but slanted." Ristinen objected to
what he considered to be some overstatements. For instance, Clayton
asserts that local fallout is more dangerous than long-term fallout,
since it settles to the ground earlier following a nuclear explosion and
therefore retains a greater level of initial radioactivity; and this assumption is apparently incorrect. But Ristinen pointed out that
"local" fallout can, after all, extend for hundreds of miles beyond the
detonation site. In short, though Clayton's basic claim is accurate, he
fails to acknowledge that the matter in question (in this case, distribution of "local" fallout) might have wider effects than he imagines.

Another scientist, Dr. Julius London, pointed out other limitations in the survivalists' data. Clayton, Kearny, and other writers
claim, for instance, that radiation passes harmlessly through air, food,
and water without making them radioactive. All in all, this is true. Fallout particles suspended in water do not mean that the water itself
becomes radioactive; however, the water may well be extremely
dangerous unless someone removes the particles before drinking it.

Thomas Nieman and other survivalists advocate the use of filters to remove the particles. This works well as far as it goes, but apparently it doesn't go far enough. London told me, "The water problem is frightfully complicated. In the event of a large war, radioactive particles would pollute all our known large water storage areas. Nobody really knows what would happen, but everybody in the scientific community says that the problem would be very, very serious. Radioactivity would infuse all our reservoirs. What would happen to the surviving population as a result?" As to the suggestion that survivors pump water from deep, unpolluted wells, Robert Ristenen asked, "How would you pump it?" The aftermath of a war might make the necessary technology unavailable or inadequate to the demand.

Information about the long-term effects of fallout presents some special problems. Bruce Clayton's data about leukemia, cancer, and genetic damage appear to be accurate. The Japanese study entitled *Hiroshima and Nagasaki,* for instance, states that "Death from leukemia among the exposed survivors has been increasing since 1947," but adds that based on current (as of 1981) studies, "the occurance of chronic lymphatic leukemia is rare in those exposed to the atomic bomb." Of malignant tumors, this study claims that they "have been shown to have a significant relation to atomic bomb exposure," but that statistical correlations remain unclear. The authors of *Hiroshima and Nagasaki* suggest that "With the accumulation of more cases and with the conclusion of the latent period of radiation carcinogenesis (causing of cancers) it may be possible to find a clear correlation to exposure in some tumors in the near future." As regards genetic problems, this study concludes that "Genetic surveys undertaken to date have yielded no positive evidence for a genetic hazard due to atomic bomb radiation," but warns, however, that "Over thirty years — only two generations — have passed since the explosion of the atomic bombs. This seems, in a sense, to be a very short interval in view of human genetics." The implication is that current data, though encouraging in light of earlier fears, remains inconclusive.

This warning holds true regarding other aspects of the issue. It is not simply a question of waiting for information to accumulate about Hiroshima and Nagasaki. The bombing of those cities has revealed much of what scientists and physicians know about how radiation effects human beings, but even thirty-five years of research may not indicate much about the consequences of a full-scale nuclear war. Survivalists and others who speculate from even the most accurate data run the risk of mistaking statistics about the past for promises about the future.

Ozone Damage

One of the most controversial issues regarding nuclear war is that of damage to the earth's ozone shield. The ozone shield — part of the atmosphere which screens the earth from ultraviolet light — appears to be vulnerable to certain effects of nuclear weapons. When a hydrogen bomb explodes, it produces enormous quantities of nitrogen oxides within its mushroom cloud; sufficient amounts of these chemicals might, under particular circumstances, reduce the ozone shield enough to let abnormal levels of ultraviolet light reach the earth's surface. The 1975 National Academy of Sciences study on nuclear weapons heightened concern that ozone damage might have major ecological consequences. Since then, scientists have debated the issue without satisfactory resolution.

Many survivalists acknowledge that some sort of controversy exists on this point, but fewer theoreticians deal with it at length than with other topics. Duncan Long makes no mention of it in his *Nuclear War Survival*. C. Bruce Sibley devotes two paragraphs of *Surviving Doomsday* to the ozone problem. Cresson Kearny omits any reference to it at all. Bruce Clayton is more attentive to the problem — though not satisfactorily so. Acknowledging that ultraviolet radiation might increase to approximately six times the present level in the aftermath of a large nuclear exchange, Clayton conjectures about the implications. "Not much is yet known about the UV threat except that some plants seem to be very sensitive to this type of light; a worldwide six-fold increase in UV light might mean extinction for many natural species, possibly including a few very important natural dominants," he writes in *Life After Doomsday*. "More serious is the fact that many agricultural crops show tremendous variation in UV sensitivity." Clayton also notes that "The UV light increase is likely to be a more serious danger to wildlife species than radiation. Many animal species are dependent upon particular plants which may die out under high UV exposure." Regarding effects on people, Clayton conceded that increase ultraviolet light poses a threat in the form of increased rates of skin cancer and severe sunburn. His conclusions:

For retreaters, the long-term effects of a nuclear war pose four direct difficulties. The first is the problem of being able to function in a high-UV envrionment. That ten-minute sunburn will be a serious nuisance. The second problem is the scalding of crops by UV light... The two or three years of abnormally cool weather will mean that a crop which does well at your retreat site under normal conditions will be unable to succeed there when the agricultural belts shift to the south. Lastly, UV-induced blindness in big game animals..will make hunting a very unproductive activity in any areas subjected to winter snows. Retreaters will have to take all these phenomena into account in their survival plans.

Elsewhere — such as in the "Nuclear Nonsense" articles Clayton dismisses the sense of danger still further. "This is what I would regard as a near-miss. The ozone question is still somewhat up in the air, but there are a few encouraging notes," and he writes in "Nuclear Nonsense, Part II." "One is that the original prediction was very shaky, what scientists would regard as an educated guess rather than an actual prediction. Second, actual measurements of ozone concentration during the period before the ban on atmospheric weapons tests did not reveal any unusual long-term effects." He concluded that "as an ecologist I find the assertions that high UV would wreak ecological havoc to be somewhat overstated."

Clayton's assertions receive some backing from the 1979 Office of Technology Assessment study of nuclear war. This OTA study notes that since 1975, when the National Academy of Science issued its report, "there have been two changes which bear on the question of the degree of risk of ozone depletion." One of these changes is further research into the chemistry of the upper atmosphere. For the most part, this new research indicates that nuclear explosions "could deplete the ozone layer if they occur at very high altitudes (80,000 ft. (24 km) and upwards) , which would result from very high-yield explosions (i.e., substantially more than 1 Mt) in large numbers (1,000 or more), or possibly from high-altitude explosions." The other change is the development of the Multiple Independent Re-entry Vehicles (MIRV) — a highly sophisticated warhead system — which, according to the OTA study, "has reduced the number of very high-yield warheads in the arsenals of the superpowers, as they are replaced by multiple weapons of lower yield." What this implies is that current technology, if employed in a nuclear war, seems less likely to damage the ozone shield even if current assumptions about atmospheric chemistry prove to be accurate.

However, Clayton and other survivalists sometimes extrapolate from this information to an unwarranted degree. Thomas Nieman told me at one point, for instance, that the ozone issue was "just hypothetical," and was therefore not one of great concern. Clayton, speaking of the OTA study in a flyer describing books he sells, writes that "This report says *the ozone layer is safe* (his italics). What the OTA study actually states is that "These changes cast doubt on the likelihood of serious ozone depletion as a consequence of nuclear war. However, they by no means demonstrate that ozone depletion is impossible, and even slight depletion could cause an increase in the incidence of skin cancer." The study concludes that "it is not possible to estimate the probability or the probable magnitude of such damage."

Survivalist writers and other persons who speculate about possible effects of nuclear was also frequently neglect to examine more that the most obvious of consequences. For example, increased ultraviolet light may cause snowblindness or other damage to human eyes, but people can protect themselves with sunglasses, visors, and other devices. What about animals though? Clayton once again downplays the danger. "Direct effects of UV on wildlife are possible, but they shouldn't be serious for most animals," he writes in *Life After Doomsday*. "With the exception of birds, most of which are helpless in the dark, I suspect that most wildlife will adopt the nocturnal pattern for a few years." He adds that most mammals are nocturnal anyway. But this is assuming a lot. Would animals readily adapt to sudden changes in the surrounding light? Would sufficient numbers of them change deeply ingrained feeding and nesting patterns to perpetuate their species? Or would they be helpless to deal with the threat? Inability to adapt might result in the blinding of millions of animals. Clayton himself suggests that birds are especially vunerable in this regard. Of course, some persons might argue that the death of wildlife is relatively inconsequental. The actual results, however, may prove catastrophic. The blinding of millions of animals might have consequences far beyond the deaths of the individual creatures. For instance, certain species of birds prey on insects; the destruction of those species might allow the insect population to surge, with potentially drastic results on the ecosystem. Similar disruptions might take place in the meantime, and not just on dry land: marine habitats, too, might suffer the effects of increased ultraviolet light. In short, ozone depletion might affect not only individual animals and plants, but also their ecological interactions. Survivalists are correct in pointing out that the issue remains inconclusive; however, the lack of a conclusion doesn't guarantee that the eventual outcome will be favorable.

Other Atmospheric Effects

Unfortunately, the problem of ozone depletion is only one of several which might affect the atmosphere following a nuclear war. Many persons — including survivalists — have acknowledged the ozone problem, yet few mention the other possibilities.

Bruce Clayton's *Life After Doomsday* is unusual in making at least passing reference to atmospheric effects other than ozone damage. One possible result of nuclear war, according to Clayton, "is the injection of nonradioactive dust into the stratosphere along with the delayed fallout. Like an immense volcanic eruption, the detonation of thousands of silo-destroying megaton weapons will put millions of tons of dust into the air," and this may in turn result in "effectively changing the clarity of the atmosphere and shading the planet's surface." Clayton adds that scientists who have studied this phenomenon have "predicted a resulting drop in average temperature of about 1 degree centigrade. The dust is expected to settle out of the air completely in two years or so."

The years since Clayton's book was published have provided time for researchers to explore questions of atmospheric effects in more detail. As with other aspects of assessing nuclear war, this one appears to be more intricate than most people first thought. The problem is not simply a matter of dust. A nuclear war would, in fact, stir up enormous quantities of dust in precisely the manner which Clayton describes; but there would be other consequences as well. One of them would be smoke and gases generated by thousands of forest fires, brush fires, and burning cities which nuclear bombs would ignite. Another would by hydrocarbon pollution from exploding oil refineries, fuel storage depots, and even oil and natural gas wells. Croplands would also burn, since many missile silos and airfields border agricultural areas both in the United States and the Soviet Union. The result would be gas and particulate pollution which could well change climatic patterns and thus alter survivors' chances of enduring the aftermath of a nuclear war.

Two scientists who have analyzed this situation are Paul J. Crutzen and John W. Birks. Crutzen, Director of the Air Chemistry Division of the Max Planck Institute for Chemistry, in Mainz, Germany, and Birks, Associate Professor of Chemistry at the University of Colorado, have recently published a study entitled "The Atmosphere After a Nuclear War: Twilight at Noon" (*Ambio* 11: 2-3, 1982). This study describes the results of a computer model based on two nuclear war scenarios. Scenario One assumes 5,750 megatons detonated, most of the weapons with yields smaller than one megaton. Scenario Two assumes 10,000 megatons detonated — 5,000 1-megaton weapons and 500 10-megaton weapons. (The authors acknowledge that this scenario doesn't reflect the most likely events in an actual nuclear war during the 1980s; but since it resembles the scenarios employed in studies like the 1975 NAS report, they have included it anyway for purposes of comparison.)

The authors conclude that "severely damaging effects to human life and the delicate ecosystems to which we belong will occur during the following weeks and months" after a nuclear war. These are in addition to possible ozone damage. In fact, Crutzen and Birks regard the risk of ozone depletion as a less drastic possibility than others. "From an atmospheric point of view," they write, "the most serious effects of a nuclear war would most likely result from the many fires which would start in the war and could not be extinguished because of nuclear contaminations and loss of water lines, fire equipment and expert personnel." They note several kinds of fires which could pollute the atmosphere. These are fires in *1)* urban and industrial areas, *2)* forests, *3)* grasslands and agricultural lands, and *4)* natural gas and oil wells. Survivalists and others may argue, of course, that neither the Soviet Union nor the United States is likely to target the other country's forests and farmlands on purpose; but this argument ignores the unintentional burning of these areas which would occur when bombs strike military and other strategic targets. The authors point out that "In the US and especially in Canada and the USSR, vast forests are found close to important urban strategic centers, so that it may be expected that many wildfires would start burning during and after the nuclear exchange." In the meantime, oil wells, refineries, and storage areas are among the likeliest of nuclear targets.

What would be the consequences of such fires? Crutzen and Birks consider the possibilities in more detail than most people would like (or would be able) to follow. Briefly, their data indicates that carbon dioxide and carbon monoxide levels would greatly increase; ozone levels might rise, "leading to global photochemical smog conditions;" particulate matter (smoke and dust) might reduce the average sunlight penetration (through the atmosphere) "by a factor between 2 and 150 at noontime in the summer;" and burning oil and gas might also become "another source of copious amounts of particulate matter in the atmosphere." They note that these events are currently speculative. However, their variables are apparently intentional underestimations: they consider the scenario to be "probably the minimum of what may occur." Yet the results of such "minimum" events actually taking place would be catastrophic.

> The fires would create sufficient quantities of airborne particulate matter in the atmosphere to screen out a large fraction of the solar radiation for many weeks, strongly reducing or even eliminating the possibility of growing agricultural crops over large areas of the Northern Hemisphere. Dark aerosol deposits would likewise severely limit plant productivity. In addition, if the war should start during the summer months, as envisaged in the war scenario of this study, much cropland would be destroyed directly by fast-moving fires.

Damage might extend well beyond even severe agricultural consequences. Crutzen and Birks state that:

> If the production of aerosol by fires is large enough to cause reductions in the penetration of sunlight to ground level by a factor of a hundred, which would be quite possible in the event of an all-out nuclear war, most of the phytoplankton and herbivorous zooplankton in more than half of the Northern Hemisphere oceans would die.

In addition, "The normal dynamic and temperature structure of the atmosphere would...change considerably over a large fraction of the Northern Hemisphere, which will probably lead to important changes in land surface temperatures and wind systems." Such changes could lead to widespread ecological disturbances.

The authors of this study concede that "Regarding possible climatic effects, little can be said with confidence." However, the short-term effects seem frightfully clear: "Under such conditions it is likely that agricultural production in the Northern Hemisphere would be almost totally eliminated, so that no food would be available for the survivors of the initial effects of the war." Crutzen and Birks add that "It is also quite possible that severe, worldwide photochemical smog conditions would develop...that would likewise interfere with plant productivity. Survival becomes even more difficult if stratospheric ozone depletions also take place." Their conclusion: "It is, therefore, difficult to see how much more than a small fraction of the initial survivors of a nuclear war in the middle and high latitude regions of the Northern Hemisphere could escape famine and disease during the following year."

Other Medical Issues

In addition to the direct medical consequences of nuclear war — traumatic injuries, radiation sickness, famine, and so forth — there are also some of a more general and indirect nature. These are the effects of inadequate equipment and personnel to care for the sick and wounded in the aftermath of a war. Most physicians, nurses, technicians, and other medical professionals reside and work in cities with populations of 50,000 or greater; and since such cities are among the places likely to be struck during a nuclear attack — or else are close enough to military targets that they would suffer from drastic side effects — a war would kill or injure thousands of precisely those persons who might otherwise have cared for survivors. In addition, blast and radiation would destroy or render useless hundreds of hospitals, clinics, and other medical facilities. Whatever staff and supplies managed to function after the attack would be inadequate for the task at hand.

Dr. Howard Hiatt, Dean of the Harvard School of Public Health, described a situation which puts this medical dilemma into perspective. In the *Journal of the American Medical Association* (244, No. 20), Hiatt writes of a car accident victim whose injuries resembled those produced by nuclear weapons. "A 20-year-old man was recently hospitalized in the burn unit of one of Boston's teaching hospitals after an automobile accident in which the gasoline tank exploded, resulting in extensive third-degree burns." During this patient's hospitalization, "he received 281 units of fresh-frozen plasma, 147 units of fresh-frozen RBC's (red blood cells), 37 units of platelets, and 36 units of albumin. He underwent six operative procedures, during which wounds involving 85 percent of his body surface were closed with homograft, cadaver allograft, and artificial skin." Hiatt states that "Throughout his hospitalization, he required mechanical ventilation and monitoring with central venous lines, arterial lines, and an intermittent pulmonary artery line. Despite these heroic measures, which stretched the resources of one of the country's most comprehensive medical institutions, he died on his 33rd hospital day." These injuries, according to Hiatt, though "conventional" in nature, reveal at least a glimpse of what post-war medical problems might involve. Yet adequate facilities and personnel simply wouldn't exist after a nuclear exchange.

The 1979 OTA study on nuclear war corroborates Hiatt's concern that the medical task following a nuclear war would exceed even the most earnest efforts. Describing one of several scenarios in the study — a single one-megaton bomb exploding over Detroit — the authors estimate that there would be 250,000 fatalities, 500,000 injuries, and severe damage to the city's medical facilities. "The near half-million injured present a medical task of incredible magnitude," states the OTA study. Of sixty-three nearby hospitals containing 18,000 beds, "55 percent of these beds are inside the 5-psi (blast overpressure) ring and thus totally destroyed. Another 15 percent in the 2- to 5-psi band will be severely damaged, leaving 5,000 beds remaining outside the region of significant damage." The study reflects on this level of destruction: "Since this is only 1 percent of the number of injured (i.e., 5,000 patients), these beds are incapable of providing significant medical assistance." The OTA authors also note that "In the first few days, transport of injured out of the damaged area will be severely hampered by debris clogging the streets. In general, only the nonprofessional assistance of nearby survivors can hope to hold down the large number of subsequent deaths that would otherwise occur."

Survivalists may argue once again that these concerns don't apply to them. Millions of Americans might well suffer the consequences of blast and intense radiation, but survivalists intend to keep their distance from nuclear targets and thus avoid the consequences. And of course they may actually succeed in doing so. Living far away from target areas would unquestionably reduce the number and severity of medical problems for some people following a nuclear war. However, even the most remote location cannot necessarily avoid all effects. The most obvious reason is that nuclear weapons may not strike their intended targets. Even the most sophisticated technology can go awry;

bombs can miss. A survivalist tucked away in the California Sierra might end up catching a MIRV intended, for, say, McClellan Air Force Base outside Sacramento. Then what? He may have a few more injured friends and relatives to nurse than he expected.

Another aspect of medical problems is less dramatic. Perhaps survivalists would escape the direct effects of a nuclear attack; and perhaps they would even avoid most long-term consequences, such as radiation. But what of indirect effects? A major nuclear war would have obliterated much or most of twentieth century civilization in the northern hemisphere — and if not forever, then at least for a few decades. All but the most optimistic survivalists acknowledge that the first several years would be brutally harsh. What sort of medicine will they practice then? Where will they obtain their supplies? From where will they acquire their skills?

Survivalists respond to these questions in various ways. Some of them rely on "handy tips"-styled medical advice of the most rudimentary kind. Duncan Long, for instance, offers bits and pieces of information in his *Nuclear War Survival*: "Pregnant women should avoid radiation as much as possible as fetuses are extremely sensitive to radiation." "Carbon monoxide poisoning produces all or some of the following: headache, vertigo, labored breathing, confusion, dilated pupils, cherry red lips, and finally convulsions and coma." "If someone in the shelter dies, the body should be removed as quickly as possible from the shelter area." Cresson Kearny goes into more detail in *Nuclear War Survival Skills*, covering topics like "Disposal of Human Wastes," "Disposal of Dead Bodies," "Clean Water and Food," "Control of Insects," "Radiation Sickness," and "Prevention of Skin Diseases." Bruce Clayton's *Life After Doomsday* is both more comprehensive and more candid than other treatments. Asking, "What would we do if we needed professional medical help and couldn't get it?" Clayton answers, "The retreaters I have met regard that possibility as the single most difficult problem they face." He then outlines possible solutions.

Some survivalists solve the problem — at least to their own satisfaction — by joining forces with a physician. Others are themselves medical practitioners. This gives them the advantage of continuous access to help in case of emergencies. Some have, in fact, become survivalists because of a general orientation toward emergency preparedness. One of these is G.G., a family practitioner in central Indiana who, along with his wife (a registered nurse), has acquired an extensive array of medicines and equipment to augment more common survival supplies. "We're optimists," G.G. says of himself and his wife, "and what we've done is aimed as much toward tornado and blizzard protection as anything else. Also, we enjoy the land. But we're also prepared for an eventuality like — God forbid — a nuclear holocaust." Their medical supplies include antibiotics, "discomfort medicines," and surgical supplies. Given their backgrounds, G.G. and his wife would undoubtedly weather most medical crises better than laypersons.

But is even this sort of preparation sufficient? Physicians, nurses, and other practitioners may be highly skilled in one set of circumstances and dangerously limited in another. Saying so doesn't insult their talents and training; it simply acknowledges the limits of human ability and the severity of the challenges facing them. A friend of mine, a young physician, brought this to my attention recently. He is an excellent cardiologist. His work presents him with many emergencies, including cardiac arrest, and he responds to them with tremendous fortitude, energy, and skill. But he also depends on an extremely elaborate backup system in hospital wards and emergency rooms: medicines, diagnostic instruments, and support staff. When an elderly acquaintance died in his presence, the young doctor was shocked by his own helplessness. "I've saved more lives than I can count — and it goes to your head after a while," he told me. "You think you can save anyone. Then somebody suffers an MI (hard attack) when you're 'off duty', and what can you do? Start CPR (cardiac resuscitation)? Great. But you're out on a fishing trip. Where's the Cor Team? Where's the 'crash cart'? There isn't any. You're alone in the woods. All you can do is keep up with the compressions (external heart massage) till you get tired and have to stop."

The risk here is simply that even medically sophisticated survivalists — who are at best a minority within the movement — may overrate their abilities in the aftermath of a nuclear war. As Bruce Clayton notes, "There are perhaps a dozen physicians in the country who have seen a case of radiation sickness." How will even first-rate doctors deal with this unfamiliar malady? Even less exotic ailments may provide insurmountable challenges in the absence of advanced technology. What if the months and years following a war prove more difficult than survivalists have imagined? What if their stockpiles of medicines, however vast, end up paltry compared to actual needs? What if a woman starts to hemorrhage after a miscarriage? What if someone accidently shoots a friend in the face? What if cholera, typhoid, and bubonic plague break out among nuclear survivors? What if ordinary old influenza turns into pneumonia during the winter? Then what?

Nobody can answer these questions adequately. Survivalists claim that their preparations would carry them through — or at least (among the more modest) that a stockpile of drugs and equipment could make a big difference. It's difficult to counter the argument that some degree of preparation is better than nothing at all. But medical problems provide one of the riskiest areas for self-delusion among survivalists.

Synergism

There is another aspect of the medical issue which deserves special note. Synergism is the cooperative action of discrete events producing a total effect greater than the sum of the separate effects, and it's pertinent to any discussion of nuclear war. This is especially true regarding the effects of a war on human beings. Unfortunately, few people acknowledge the issue at all. Of the various studies, only the OTA's *The Effects of Nuclear War* examines synergism in any detail.

"So far the discussion of each major effect (blast, nuclear radiation, and thermal radiation) has explained how this effect in isolation causes deaths and injuries to humans," write the OTA authors of their analysis. They note that their own and other studies most often consider the effects of nuclear weapons in this manner: one at a time. However, this is a less realistic way of calculating the effects of an actual war. The problem is that estimating the consequences of more than one variable at a time limits the accuracy of most projections. (The more variables, the less accuracy.) "It is obvious that combined injuries are possible, but there are no generally accepted ways of calculating their probability," the authors state. They conjecture about some of the likliest combinations anyway.

Nuclear radiation combined with thermal radiation. "It is clear from experiments with laboratory animals that exposure of a burn victim to more than 100 rems of radiation will impair the blood's ability to support recovery from thermal burns," according to the OTA study. The implication is that a sublethal radiation dose might prevent a burn victim from recovering after suffering an otherwise survivable burn.

Nuclear radiation combined with mechanical injuries. The OTA writers list a variety of injuries (such as puncture wounds from flying glass, broken bones from blast effects, and cuts from collapsing structures) which radiation would aggravate. "There is evidence," the authors note, "that all of these types of injuries are more serious if the person has been exposed to 300 rems, particularly if treatment is delayed. Blood damage (from radiation) will clearly make a victim more susceptible to blood loss and infection.

Thermal radiation and mechanical injuries. Although "There is no information available about the effects of this combination," the OTA assumes that "Mechanical injuries should be prevalent at about the distance from a nuclear explosion that produces sublethal burns," and that the combination of injuries might therefore "subject the body to a total stress that it cannot tolerate."

The authors therefore conclude that "Because the uncertainties of nuclear effects are compounded when one tries to estimate the likelihood of two or more serious but (individually) nonfatal injuries, there is really no way to estimate the number of victims." As in other respects, however, this doesn't mean that they wouldn't exist. Moreover, the OTA study points out that "A further dimension of the problem is the possible synergism between injuries and environmental damage." An obvious example they offer is that "poor sanitation (due to the loss of electrical power and water pressure) can clearly compound the effects of any kind of serious injury." Another possibility — one not considered by the OTA — is the combination of injury and inadequate food supply. It's worth noting also that two variables is hardly the maximum number possible. People might end up injured, burned, irradiated, malnourished, and even deprived of water — all at the same time. Even survivalists who managed to escape these effects of war by virtue of their remote locations might have to struggle against the synergism of illness, bad weather, and long-term threats to their wellbeing in the shape of other survivalists.

Psychological Issues

Lastly — and most often neglected — is the issue of psychological consequences. Commentators often explore the effects of nuclear war on the body without considering any possible effects on the mind. A few survivalist theoreticians touch on what they call "survival psychology" or "mental conditioning" in their books: Mel Tappan, for instance, mentions the benefits of Transcendental

Meditation on the ability to concentrate. Rank and file survivalists sometimes speak of the stresses and hardships they anticipate following a disaster. But nobody within the survival movement (at least to my knowledge) has explored the psychological dimensions of surviving a nuclear war.

The reason is simple. As with other efforts at predicting what might hapen, this one requires drawing conclusions from limited data; but unlike more quantifiable phenomena, the workings of the human mind rarely lend themselves to precise conclusions. Few events provide a setting for psychological study of this sort. There has never been a war comparable even to "limited" nuclear exchange between the superpowers. The only wartime use of atomic weapons has been the bombing of Hiroshima and Nagasaki — catastrophes which would appear small compared to the devastation following a mid-Eighties nuclear war. As a result, estimating the psychological consequences of such a war becomes highly speculative.

There are nonetheless a few individuals who have undertaken the task. One of them is Robert Jay Lifton, M.D., a professor of psychiatry at the Yale University School of Medicine. Lifton's 1967 book, *Death in Life* was the first to study the effects of nuclear devstation on the human psyche. By interviewing survivors of the Hiroshima and Nagasaki bombings, Lifton explores both "the indelible imprint of the event and its endlessly reverberating psychological repercussions." The result is one of the most insightful views into this complex subject. More recently, Lifton has written about what the Japanese experience during the Second World War suggests about the future.

"Scenarios' about fighting, recovering from, or even 'winning' a nuclear war tend to be remarkably vague about the psychological condition of survivors," Lifton notes in a *New York Times* article entitled "Nuclear War's Efect on the Mind" (March 15, 1982). "Some commentators simply assume that survivors will remain stoic and begin to rebuild from the ruins in a calm, disciplined way. Others seem to attribute that rebuilding to a mysterious, unseen hand." Lifton claims that "Usually absent is a reasoned estimate, on the basis of what experience we have, of how people might actually be expected to behave."

"Recently," he goes on to say, "physicians and other scientists have been making careful projections of the effects of nuclear war, and all raise severe doubts about general claims of recovery." Some of these projections originate from studies of actual catastrophes, among them the bombings of Hiroshima and Nagasaki.

In Hiroshima, survivors not only expected that they too would soon die; they had a sense that *everyone* was dying, that "the world is ending." Rather than panic, the scene was one of slow motion — of people moving gradually away from the center of the destruction, but dully and almost without purpose. They were, as one among them put it, "so broken and confused that they moved and behaved like automatons...a people who walked in the realm of dreams." Some tried to do something to help others, but most felt themselves to be so much part of a dead world that, as another remembered, they were "not really alive."

Lifton notes that "The key to that vague behavior was a closing off of the mind so that no more horror could enter it. People witnessed the most grotesque forms of death and dying all around them but felt nothing." Instead, "A profound blandness and insensitivity — a 'paralysis of the mind' — seemed to take hold in everyone."

Lifton points out, however, that even the disasters at Hiroshima and Nagasaki "can provide us with no more than a hint of what would happen in the event of a nuclear war...In a nuclear war, the process of psychic numbing may well be so extreme as to become irreversible." The reason is that the suddenness and extent of a war "would not give the survivors any chance to mobilize the usual forms of psychological defense. The normal human response to mass death and profound horror is not rage or depression or panic or mourning or even fear;" instead, it is "a kind of mental anesthetization that interferes with both judgement and compassion for other people." The psychological consequences of a nuclear war may extend beyond the effects of "ordinary" human calamity. Lifton notes that even minor disasters — a flood, an earthquake, a fire — produce this protective immobilization. "But in the event of a nuclear attack, the immobilization may reach the point where the psyche is no longer connected to its own past and is, for all practical purposes, severed from the social forms from which it drew strength and a sense of humanity." Lifton imagines this resulting in a bizarre scene: "The landscape is almost moon-like, spare and quiet, and the survivors who root among the ruins seem to have lost contact with one another, not to mention the ability to form cooperating groups and offer warmth and solace to people around them."

Of course, most survivors — no matter how badly dislocated by a natural disaster or a war — eventually come to their senses and return to the task of living. But Lifton suggests that "In most cases...that

sense of isolation quickly disappears with the realization that the rest
of the world is still intact. The disaster, it turns out, is local, confined,
bounded." Rescue teams show up; neighbors or allies or even occupy-
ing armies (as in the case of World War II) come and help the
destitute to recover; individuals and communities renew themselves.
"That sense of communion, that perception that the textures of social
existence remain more or less whole, is a very important part of the
healing that follows," according to Lifton. But he adds: "None of that
will happen in a nuclear war." With the decimation of whole nations
and the severing of transportation from any countries left relatively
unscathed, "There will be no surrounding human community, no un-
damaged world out there to count on. There will be no succor outside
— no infusion of the vitality, the confidence in the continuity of left,
the disaster victims have always needed so desperately."

The result would be a disaster beyond the scope of our imaginations. Lifton expects that "survivors will remain in a deadened state,
either alone or among others like themselves, largely without hope
and vaguely aware that everyone and everything that once mattered to
them has been destroyed." Since the consenquences of a nuclear war
would produce not only individual trauma, but a collective form as
well, "The bonds that link people in connecting groups will be badly
torn, in most cases irreparably, and their behavior is likely to become
muted and accompanied by suspiciousness and extremely primitive
forms of thought and action." Lifton concludes that the truism to the
effect that *"The living will envy the dead"* after a nuclear war may in
fact prove untrue — but not for the reasons which some people have
claimed. Survivors "would be incapable of such feelings. They would
not so much envy as, inwardly and outwardly, resemble the dead."

Survivalists would (and in fact already do) take issue with most
of the matters discussed in this chapter. The most perceptive among
them, such as Kearny and Clayton, often agree that yes, the danger is
great, the task of survival is arduous, the outcome is uncertain; but
they also argue that information, hard work, and optimism will help
them to prevail. Others base their actions on a more intuitive scheme
of things. They simply assume that somehow they will make it
through the holocaust. They are the new Noahs. They are the Chosen
Few. They are the remnant which will endure the collapse of the present age and will inherit the new age to come. The convictions vary;
the basic assumption does not. Survivalists expect to live through a
nuclear war.

Does the available evidence support this expectation? This is, of course, both the most important question concerning survivalism and also the most difficult. Accumulating information is a complex task; drawing conclusions from it is something else entirely. When predicting the outcome of nuclear war, even identifying all the variables becomes impossible. How many bombs will explode? What will their yields be? Will they be airbursts or groundbursts? When will they strike? During the day or at night? In winter, spring, summer, fall? Will they explode over the course of a few hours? A few days? Weeks? Months? As the variables increase in number, the accuracy of *any* prediction drops. This is true even — especially — with computer models. Much of the information available is speculative anyway. Of course, two precedents exist: Hiroshima and Nagasaki. Ignoring those cities and what happened to them is both tempting and impossible, and the experience of their citizens may tell us more about nuclear reality than we care to know. But as Julius London pointed out to me, "The difference (between the Hiroshima and Nagasaki bombings and what could happen now) is so large that is is not possible to make comparisons." The result is that nobody really knows what would happen as a result of a nuclear war.

Still, it would be dangerous to ignore the extrapolations currently available. They may not explain everything, but they offer a point of reference. They also offer a context for examining survivalists' claims about their chances of surviving a nuclear war relatively unscathed.

Three documents offer credible predictions about the aftermath of a nuclear war: the NAS study already mentioned; the OTA study; and a 1982 book entitled *Life After Nuclear War*, by Arthur M. Katz. All three of these studies conclude that the human race would survive even a full-scale nuclear war, though with varying assessments of the probable damage. All three also qualify their conclusions by warning against the temptation to regard this outcome as "encouraging."

The NAS study, for instance — confined to research on "more distant peoples and ecosystems" than those within the combatant nations — concludes that the biosphere and the species *Homo sapiens* would survive. "Reasoning from available information and understanding," writes Philip Handler, President of the NAS, in his introduction, "it is concluded that, a decade or so after the event, in areas distant from the detonations, surviving humans and ecosystems would be subject to relatively minimal stress attributable to the exchange."

He adds, however, that although the damage may seem less drastic than many persons have feared, these consequences makes sense "only on a relative scale. The economic, social, and political consequences of the resultant worldwide terror are entirely unpredictable."

In contrast, the OTA study goes into detail on how nuclear war would affect the combatant nations, and it examines long-term global effects more briefly than the NAS study does. Its general conclusions are that:

1. "The effects of a nuclear war that cannot be calculated are at least as important as those for which calculations are attempted." This includes effects such as lack of adequate medical care for survivors, economic damage, and unpredictable damage to the environment.

2. "The impact of even a 'small' or 'limited' nuclear attack would be enormous." Deaths from an attack restricted to oil refineries and limited merely to ten missiles, for instance, would produce more than five million fatalities in the United States. Other "limited" attacks might kill up to twenty million people.

3. "Although it is true that effective sheltering and/or evacuation could save lives, it is not clear that a civil defense program based on providing shelters or planning evacuation would necessarily be effective." The OTA study emphasizes the need for food, water, medical supplies, and other critical goods to support a population after the attack; shelter alone is insufficient. In addition, the authors note that "The effectiveness of civil defense measures depends, among other things, on the events leading up to the attack, the enemy's targeting policy, and sheer luck."

4. "The situation in which the survivors of a nuclear attack find themselves will be quite unprecedented." Noting that a war would destroy natural resources, equipment, and even agricultural lands, the OTA study concluded that "The surviving nation would be far weaker — economically, socially, and politically — than one would calculate by adding up the surviving economic assets and the numbers and skills of the surviving people."

5. Lastly, the study notes that "From an economic point of view, and possibly from a political and social viewpoint as well, conditions after an attack would get worse before they started to get better." The

implication here is that for a while after the war, "people could live off supplies (and, in a sense, off habits) left over from before the war. But shortages and uncertainties would get worse." As a result, survivors would have to race against time to achieve economic viability — with production at least equaling consumption plus depreciation of stored goods — in order to re-establish an economy. "A failure to achieve viability, or even a slow recovery," the authors note, "would result in many additional deaths, and much additional economic, political, and social deterioration. This postwar damage could be as devastating as the damage from the actual nuclear explosions."

Arthur Katz's *Life After Nuclear War* is the most recent study on the subject, hence the one most attuned to the current balance of nuclear power in the world. (The NAS study, for instance, though still significant, is less accurate now than it was in 1975: both the United States and the Soviet Union have changed certain weapons systems and, to a lesser extent, certain nuclear strategies.) Katz reaches a conclusion similar to what the NAS and OTA stated in the reports, however. "It is important to make the observation that there will be many survivors in the world, and even in the nations directly involved in a nuclear war," he states. "Nuclear war may indeed have the appearance of Armageddon, but it is distinctly not the end of the world. However, for those nations involved in a nuclear exchange it may be the end of *their* world." Even "surviving" a nuclear war may involve a calamitous outcome. Katz suggests that "After an attack using weapons with the destructive power of only a few hundred megaton equivalents, the United States, Soviet Union, or other countries may resemble underdeveloped nations lurching from one economic and political crisis to another." Since a nuclear exchange involving a few hundred megatons would be extremely small by contemporary standards — U.S. and Soviet arsenals, according to *Time* magazine (March 29,1982), contain an estimated 11,373 megatons of destructive force — the likelihood is that consequences would be vastly worse than what Katz describes.

What these various studies indicate is that survivalists and others may well be correct in their asusmptions that somehow the human race would survive. Most information supports this claim. However, three problems complicate the situation. One is that current information may not cover all eventual effects of nuclear war; there may be consequences not yet identified. Two, currently know phenomena may turn out to be more destructive than assumed. (An example of this is the effect of dust, smoke, and hydrocarbons which Birks and Crutzen discuss in their *Ambio* article.) Three, the numbers of nuclear weapons continues to increase, thereby influencing at least the quantitative degree of damage resulting from a war. The available information may, in short, prove insufficient for predicting the outcome of a war.

This brings up another issue. *Which* war? Despite the persuasive qualities of nuclear war "scenarios," they are, after all, strictly theoretical, and even the highest-ranking military officers in the nuclear nations can only speculate about what would take place in a real war. Would the United States and the Soviet Union warn each other with a chess-like series of moves and countermoves — one bomb or a few bombs at a time? Would the two countries attack each other's military installations but avoid an all-out war? Would they let everything fly at once? Would other countries join in the frenzy? European nations? China? And would the conflict end almost as soon as it began — a "spasm war"? Or would it continue after the initial attacks — one vengeful salvo after another? Some people believe that neither the Soviets nor the Americans would let a conflict go past the "counterforce" (military targets only) stage; others assume that any exchange, no matter how limited at first, would quickly escalate into all-out war. But clearly the intensity of the conflict, its duration, and the kind of targets involved would make an enormous difference on how survivalists or anyone else could live through it.

If the United States and the Soviet Union attacked each other's missile silos and bomber bases and command centers but somehow managed to hold back from more widespread destruction, then millions of Americans and Russians would survive — with or without extensive preparations. (The OTA estimates that some twenty million Americans would die.) Survivalists would no doubt manage better than their non-survivalist neighbors. The same outcome might result from a limited attact on industrial facilities, power plants, dams, and other targets of economic significance. However, a full-scale nuclear war would be another matter. The level of initial damage would be greater; the "local" fallout would be more abundant; the long-term effects — including climatic changes, disruption of agriculture, and the like — would be more severe. Even the most elaborate survival preparations might well prove insufficient for dealing with the aftermath of total nuclear war.

Survivalists will argue that such uncertainties make preparation more important, not less so. No one knows the likelihood of nuclear war, let alone what shape it will take: all the more reason to be ready for anything. If crops won't grow, then stash more food. If UV exposure will be dangerous, then set aside some dark glasses and sunscreen. If the climate turns frigid, then pack away some extra coats. An ounce of prevention is worth a pound of cure. A stitch in time saves nine. Every new threat prompts a self-respecting survivalist to find something to protect him from it. And in a way, there's a certain logic to this attitude. One certainly won't be *better* off unprepared. But will this be enough? Will the survivalists' preparations see them through?

The indications, all in all, are that the survivalists — or some of them, at least, along with some lucky non-survivalists — may end up surviving a nuclear war. Their shelters, their food, their CB equipment, their medical supplies, their decontamination gear, even their guns and ammunition: all their emergency goods may hold them in good stead and help them survive the catastrophe they anticipate. Those who prepared may live to congratulate themselves for their insight and cleverness and hard work. The Ants may outlive the Grasshoppers. The survivalists may, in fact, turn out to be the pioneers in the post-nuclear wilderness. The survivalists may end up winning when all the rest of us have lost.

Yet if so, this will have been a Pyrrhic victory. They will have survived, but at a cost higher than almost anyone had imagined. No matter, some will say; anything to survive. As one young man told me, "I'd rather become a Genghis Khan than to succumb to anything." Most survivalists remain more ethically imaginative than this. But the message is clear.

The world is sick, dying, doomed. It's time to bail out.

Chapter Eight

Conclusion:
The Question of Community

Not long ago, one of my closest friends told me, "I can't shake the feeling that the roof is going to fall in. I can't help but wonder if we're not in a situation like Europe right before the Second World War. You know that trouble is on the way, but somehow you never get around to doing anything about it. Some of my relatives did: they left. But most of them didn't. They waited and waited, and then it was too late." My friend is Jewish; like many American Jews, she lost family members in the Holocaust. The weight of that loss lingers a long while — years, decades, a whole lifetime, generations. And so she spoke of her fears and wondered what to do about them. "Perhaps it's time to clear out," she added.

But clear out *where?* I asked her. We discussed the possibilities for a whole evening. To Europe? What kind of escape hatch would that be? Soviet military planners have approximately 1200 prime targets in Europe (according to Nigel Calder in *Nuclear Nightmares*), and bombing them would result in some 150 million deaths — half the population of the NATO nations. South America? Africa? Asia? These continents, though not as likely to suffer direct attack, wouldn't escape all the consequences of a major nuclear war. Fallout would reach even the remotest areas of the globe. Although its intensity would have diminished, radiation from delayed fallout might well present a long-term threat to health. Other problems would create more immediate dangers: climatic changes and complex forms of ecological damage. If nothing else, the effects of a nuclear war on the world economy — with or without disruption of agriculture — could produce famine throughout many Third World countries. How about Australia, then? Or New Zealand? These seemed like the likeliest candidates. Unfortunately, these nations would not necessarily escape the indirect consequences of a nuclear war; and they might, in addition, suffer direct attack as well.

My friend and I never decided on what she should do. I was skeptical of her chances for getting away. During the last years of the Weimar Republic, people could leave Europe for the United States, for Canada, for Palestine...Now there was no safe place. At least there was no place which anyone *knows* will be safe.

Yet I sympathized with her, and told her so. Even children (of remarkably young age, too) know that the world is in dangerous shape these days. Only the oblivious, the naive, and the self-deluding fail to acknowledge the danger. What's more, the impulse to escape is natural — simply a part of being human. Who doesn't want to survive? Even the survivalist agenda seems predictable given the current tangle of problems in the world. It seems like a way of cutting the Gordian Knot. Not just misanthropes, but also responsible, ethically sensitive, gregarious people can easily wonder if staying put isn't a form of sucide. But it it? And is survivalism really the alternative it seems? I mean this in a broader sense than just, "Will it work?" Are there possibly some other issues, a broader context, which the survival movement fails to address? Survivalists often speak of themselves as the industrious, responsible Ants who go about their business while the foolish Grasshoppers waste their time. Another popular image is that of the ostrich: survivalists claim to recognize the dangers surrounding them while other people stick their heads in the sand. But perhaps these symbols are inadequate. There's the possibility that survivalism, though outwardly acknowledging the nuclear dilemma, in fact avoids dealing with it on any but the most superficial level.

Even some observers who remain skeptical about survivalists, and who regard their activities as counterproductive, nonetheless see the movement as part of a more general phenomenon. Robert Jay Lifton, for example, has tried to make sense of survivalist beliefs and preparations. When I asked him to share his insights in this regard, he explained, "I think that some kind of fundamental process is present here. There's a common element in survivalists, civil defense advocates, and those of us who favor disarmament: fear. What does one do with one's fear of nuclear war? So we should start with the assumption that there is common fear. People have to seek some way of dealing with it. Most of us go about maintaining various sorts of illusions about nuclear war — that it simply can't happen, or that it can't effect us. My own sense of things is that the survivalists are still clinging to nuclear illusions — that they can survive. But presumably they have faced the situation to some degree. Once you give up those illusions — once you start to understand what could happen — your fears can readily increase. At least that is the usual psychological dynamic. And the pressure then increases as well."

Lifton notes that "There's actually a close connecting link between militant anti-nuclear advocates and survivalists — not just the common fear, but even how some of them respond to it. Many anti-nuclear people have entertained the idea of going to Australia and setting up a safer life. A number of people (in the anti-nuclear camp) have considered ways to give their families a better way of surviving. If you share with some intensity the truth of nuclear danger, it's possible to swing either way. There's a tone in survivalist imagery which suggests that survivalists could swing into the anti-nuclear camp, too. a *significant* number could swing that way: but they would have to find a sense of true security in this. As for what puts them in the camp of the survivalists, I have no easy answer for this."

Other observers who have followed the survival movement through its recent stages of development see some possible explanations for what puts people "in the camp of the survivalists."

According to Henry Coppolillo, M.D., Professor of Psychiatry at the University of Colorado Medical School, "Human beings live by means of some complex regulatory mechanisms. These are partly moral, but I mean psychological mechanisms for the most part. These mechanisms are very complex. Right now, we're going through a phase in human development where artificially imposed regulation — laws — don't work the way they used to. I'm referring to social expectations also. There's a loosening of social ties, bonds, and the sense of commitment. During the past forty or fifty years, psychology and law have been moving from being a backup for the regulatory mechanisms to being the mechanisms themselves. There's a greater range of behaivor possible now than before — including some which is socially unacceptable. But the fact is that there's no way that psychology or law can regulate the human condition."

"The ways in which people coexist with each other are in rather delicate balance. One way of maintaining the balance is by identifying with people around you. There's a sense of what is appropriate behavior and what isn't. How we perceive others makes a big difference in our own thoughts and actions. These are the external cues we take in. Then there the internal cues: thoughts, fears, desires. The interplay between the external and the internal cues is important, and it is an important means of an individual regulating himself.

"One of the problems with this the survivalists' situation is that it can produce a skewed attitude." I asked Coppolillo at this point if he were referring to sociopathic behavior — antisocial attitudes or actions. He said, "Let's just say 'skewed' for the time being. I'm referring to an overly suspicious or narrowly group-centered view. My point is that in a setting with this skewed view of what the world is like, what will regulate behavior? The risk is mob psychology. Under these circumstances, there will be changes by virtue of what these people perceive around them. All of us have the potential for antisocial behavior. But without the balance maintained by being around other people — the wider community — problems can evolve in a matter of months."

How does Coppolillo explain these changes? How does he explain, for instance, the survivalists' disengagement from the wider society around them? Their conviction that they will survive despite enormous threats to them? Their willingness (at times) to survive at almost any cost?

"It's not difficult to explain," he told me. "I can tell you about something similar from my own experience. I was in the American landing at Iwo Jima. I can remember wading ashore with the Second Marines — shells bursting around me — and literally pushing the bodies aside that were floating around me. And yet I never once thought that *I* would be killed? I was convinced that I was invincible. And you know why? Because my mother wouldn't allow it. I was eighteen years old at the time. The mind works that way; it has to in order to protect itself. It's a delusion that there's no possibility of death. And something like this is at work with the survivalists. Not *just* with them — it's something which all of us do to some degree — but with them as well. People simply cannot grasp the enormity of what we're dealing with."

I then asked Coppolillo what he would anticipate in a world following a nuclear war. Assuming that people survived in groups or families, what would their lives be like?

"Whatever happens, it will not be society as we know it today. Within weeks or months, values of the sort we live by would disappear. The struggle to survive would guarantee it." When I asked him specifically what sorts of values would disappear, he told me, "Preservation of others' lives. Basic trust. Optimism. Every human engagement would be predicated on self-centered, materialistic concerns, and this would not allow what we consider normal human interaction. There would also be a focus on rights outside the context of responsibility — what you do becomes what you can get away with. Even within groups, the divisive elements might kill each other off." What would he expect if some groups managed to stay intact and cooperate within their own ranks? "I imagine that there would be a great sense of isolation. Groups would develop in their own ways, and the mores of individual groups would prevent their coalescing with other groups. Throughout history, very few groups have amalgamated when geographically separated from each other for a long period of time. This would disrupt any sense of wider affiliation. It would disrupt intellectual or emotional intimacy. And it would disrupt a sense of the future."

A psychiatrist who takes an even dimmer view of survivalism is John E. Mack, M.D. Mack, a professor of psychiatry at the Harvard Medical School, has studied people's attitudes toward the nuclear threat and how it affects contemporary society. Speaking of the survivalists, he says, "These people seem not to be raving maniacs or psychopaths," but the problem, in Mack's assessment, resembles what Copplillo perceives: they tend "to be very much focused on a conception of humanity which is limited to 'me and my world.' It's a kind of rugged individualism." Like Lifton and Coppolillo, Mack sees the problem as essentially one of trying to ignore a frightening situation — nuclear war — and to vent the anxiety this generates by taking action which appears to address the problem. "The impression the survivalists foster is that nuclear survival belongs in the realm of ordinary survival. You have articles (in survivalist magazines, for instance) about nuclear war next to articles about survival in the desert. It helps people to deny the magnitude of the danger. The reality (of nuclear war) is unacceptable; therefore, people negate the facts."

The result of this is the potential for enormous harm. Neither Mack nor Lifton nor Coppolillo regarded the survivalists as evil in an active, malicious sense; nonetheless, the potential for harm is there. Mack put this most emphatically: "It (survivalism) is sinister because people don't want to deal with painful reality. Survivalism helps them avoid it. People do this all the time (i.e., avoiding difficult or threatening situations under normal, day-to-day circumstances). Normal people use primitive (psychological) mechanisms all the time. We all do this, including when we have to think about nuclear war. The point is that in order really to survive, people need to take responsibility for facing this nuclear reality which is so scary, and shouldn't succumb to fatalism — shouldn't assume that war is inevitable. The result of survivalism is that a lot of people who aren't working to prevent nuclear war are deceiving others by helping them think they can avoid the problem."

The observations, though varied in how they stress particular issues, nevertheless share some general misgivings. All in all, the shared conclusion is that survivalists' attitudes and activities suffer from a narrow view of community. This narrow view is problematic in its own right: it attempts to exclude people from the individual's environment in ways which are no longer possible. Modern communications and transportation have rendered the world both much bigger and much smaller than it was in the past. Dismissing billions of human beings in favor of a provinvial scheme of things — myself, my family, my little group against everybody else — attempts to negate the reality of life in the late twentieth century. In addition, this effort may well aggravate already serious problems.

It is important to note that the question of community is considerably more substantial than it seems. It's not just a matter of neighborliness, though it's often assumed to be the same thing. Rather, it's a matter of what might be called human ecology. The choices which people make and the actions which they take can affect other people, and often do; and in a densely populated, highly technological world, the relationships between causes and effects are much more intricate and more powerful than most of us care to acknowledge. These relationships are also frequently unsettling and even frightening. More often than not, they challege us in ways which we find uncomfortable. The fact remains that we can ignore them only at our own peril. An example: acid rain. the policies of American industries regarding their smokestack emissions affect the pH (relative acidity or alkalinity) of rain, and this in turn can harm agriculture and wildlife throughout areas downwind of factories. Acid rain has killed fish in many northeastern lakes, and it damages forests as well. The effects on human beings are at least indirect — disrupted livelihoods, a despoiled environment. As a result, people have the responsibility of correcting the situation, but the task extends far beyond the limits of state borders and professional ties. The industrialist in Ohio and the potato farmer in Maine are, in this sense, members of the same community.

The same holds true in more drastic circumstances. Since 1945, the world has faced the prospect of nuclear war. The actual dangers have varied from year to year and from crisis to crisis, but the possibility has remained with us all along. A general consensus currently suggests that most people in the United States regard nuclear war as likely. According to a recent poll (*Newsweek*, October 5, 1981), 68% of American citizens believe that there is some chance, a good chance, or near-certainty of a nuclear war between the U.S. and the U.S.S.R. within the next ten years. And of course this fear is precisely what prompts many people to become survivalists. Nuclear war, they say, is inevitable; there's no hope but to prepare for the crunch. It's hard to blame them for this sort of pessimism. The catch is that however understandable, it is inadequate as a response. It relies on a conception of community which at best ignores the problem and at worst, aggravates it.

Three aspects of the question of community deserve special attention. They are what we might call "the dark side" of community. Few people (including survivalists) examine them, and yet they influence the choices which all of us end up making. For lack of better labels, these aspects might be called the problem of restlessness, the problem of cultural restraint, and the problem of thanatophilia.

Glenn Gray, and American philosopher who died in 1977, summed up the problem of restlessness more eloquently than anyone else. Gray's book *The Warriors* examines the psychology, morality, and even aesthetics of war, but it also considers these aspects of the *absence* of war. Despite the revulsion which most people have toward war, Gray recognized a strange attraction as well. "There is in many today as great a fear of a sterile and unexciting peace of a great war," Gray wrote in *The Warriors*. "We are often puzzled by our continued failure to enlist in the pursuit of a peaceful world the unified effort, cheerfulness in sacifice, determination, and persistence that arise almost spontaneously in the pursuit of war." Noting that most people prefer not to examine the reason for this puzzlement, Gray goes on to state that "The majority of us. restless and unfulfilled, see no supreme worth in our present state. We want more out of life than we are getting and are always half-ready to chance everything on the realization of great expectations." This can give rise to intense dissatisfaction. "Though most of us do not know what we expect of life, we reject inwardly the fate present existence has in store for us: isolation, petty routines, the stale entrapments society sets for us." The result — at least potentially — is a peculiar temptation. "It is this crushing disappointment of our confident expectations that makes us welcome a chance to exercise the military virtues, to escape into adventure, to feel the genuine excitement of the communal and the sacrificial."

Many people, among them survivalists, will protest this analysis. They don't want more trouble, more risk, more danger! All they want is survival! But the fact remains that many survivalists betray precisely the restlessness and dissatisfaction which Gray describes. This isn't to say they they want trouble — least of all disaster. The emotions involved are both subtler and more complex than that. Instead, it's a sense that the American dream has gone bad, the world has begun to degenerate, and no amount of tinkering, boot-strapping, and muddling through can make enough difference now. The most extreme for of this, of course is the current wave of apocalyptic sentiment. The End Times have arrived. Prepare to meet thy doom! As Christian survivalist Jim McKeever puts it in *Christians Will Go through the Tribulation*, "I would have to conclude that there is a high probability that we are living in the last days of this present age, and could well see the return of Christ." Millions of fundamentalists in this country would agree with McKeever's assessment. But even people with less specific expectations nonetheless feel that something has to give. "Things just can't keep up like this," many survivalists have told me. Often this attitude produces a sense of resignation: we might as well get it over with. Sometimes people even express a kind of longing for the crush.

In *The Warriors*, Glenn Gray admits that he, too — despite a thoughtful cast of mind — succumbed to these temptations. "And I have no reason to believe that my case is unique or singular," he wrote of his youthful desire that a momentous event might transform his humdrum existence. After the Second World War, he noticed the same sentiments in others, at times in the least likely persons. He relates an event which took place in 1955. Gray encountered a French woman who had suffered during the war but who now lived comfortably with her husband and son. Reviewing the hardships of the war, the woman abruptly explained that somehow, despite everything, "those times had been more satisfying than the present. 'My life is so unutterably boring nowadays!' she cried out. 'Anything is better than to have nothing at all happen day to day.'" And she told Gray, "You know that I do not love war or want it to return. But at least it made me feel alive, as I have not felt alive before or since."

Gray's reflections suggest that these emotions are normal in many ways — a common response to ambiguity or stasis. Are they therefore adequate in the face of present dangers? Would the challenge of survival in a postwar environment offer the stimulation and excitement which many people seem to desire? If Gray's analysis gives any indication, many survivors would, in fact, rise to the occasion, and they might actually experience a kind of thrill at surmounting the obstacles before them. Certainly the history of humankind is full of tales about brave men and women enduring hardship. But how long could this exhilaration last? Months? Years? Decades? All the the most sanguine survivalists admit that a massive nuclear war would end civilization as we know it. Even those survivors who managed to set up some kind of alternate economic system — subsistence farming, perhaps — would face arduous demands on their physical and emotional energies for the rest of their lives. Perhaps those who long for the simple bucolic life should give it a test run before dismissing modern society. And I don't mean organic gardening somewhere in southwest Oregon. Given likely conditions after a nuclear war, the surroundings, climate, diet, and longevity of peasants in the Peruvian Andes might provide a better sense of what's to come.

Then there is the problem of cultural restraint. Survivalists, like almost everyone else in this country, express concern that the basic substance of American society appears to be deteriorating. Some of these concerns are the age-old complaints that nobody respects authority anymore, children don't behave, and so forth. Others are specific and legitimate worries about the collapse of values and a growing sense that "anything goes." Crime spreads like a plague. Civility vanishes. People care only about their own wellbeing. Survivalists aren't the only Americans who fear that their country will slide into pandemonium. They aren't alone, either, in wanting to escape the consequences. But few of them realize that their beliefs and actions, far from differing from the sociopathic elements which they hold in contempt, often resemble them.

An example is the common practice among survivalists of acquiring elaborate weapons. Most members of the survival movement — as Bruce Clayton and other spokespersons have noted — are scarcely the gun fanatics which the popular media accuse them of being. But the militant minority is another matter. Although still fairly small, this sub-group seems influential beyond its numbers. Even survivalists who resent the militants sometimes emulate them unintentionally. Moderate survivalists, fearing the more extreme factions, acquire armaments which they might have declined to purchase otherwise. Clayton himself — the most thoughtful of survivalist writers — told me, "There's a little arms race going on now." This situation may well deteriorate futher. Relatively cautious self-protection may degenerate into outright vigilantism. American history has plenty of precedents for this; in fact, the traditions of rugged individualism and frontier ethics which many survivalists admire may end up providing a dramatic (though regrettable) model. The fact remains that current attitudes about guns can lead to tragedy. Bearing arms may be every American's right, but acquiring massive stockpiles of weapons and ammunition is more than just an expression of constitutional freedom. It's also a sign of a basically adversary attitude toward other human being. Even a relatively small crisis might transform this us-against-them orientation into chaos far beyond even the most paranoid survivalist's fantasies.

But the question of personal defense is only one of several which stem from the easing of cultural restraint. Others involve even more fundamental taboos. The fears which survivalists themselves express about "marauders" provide an indication of the problem. A growing number of people worry that some survivalists may take advantage of social breakdown to prey on others. The frequent expressions of concern about predatory human beings in Clayton's *Survivalist Directory* is one sign of this worry. A few survivalists, meanwhile, actually indicate their willingness to take advantage of the situation after a disaster. Those who question the likelihood of this happening should reflect on the incidence of pillage, rape, and other forms of wanton violence in the aftermath of wars and social breakdowns throughout history.

At times, people express their inclinations with remarkable frankness. A correspondent to the *Long Survival Newsletter* (III, No. 3, 1982), for instance, wrote that "My question is perhaps a little bizarre: do you know of any publication that deals factually with cannibalism? I think that in a time of world-wide catastrophe and food shortage, cannibalism would be perhaps one of the best ways to sustain oneself." The editor, Duncan Long, responds by dismissing the idea. "Our advice on cannibalism is to forget it. There are a number of problems which are insurmountable as far as we are concerned with the practice of cannibalism." Long then proceeds to explain his reservations. But he concluded, "An interesting idea. New ideas are needed but cannibalism would certainly seem to be a counterproductive survival strategy."

Lastly — but certainly related to these other problems — is the problem of thanatophilia. In its most extreme manifistation, this takes an especially bizarre shape. It's a state of mind in which people not only cease dreading the outbreak of war, and not only anticipate what Glenn Gray calls "the genuine excitement of the communal and the sacrificial," but also long for the finality and simplicity of obliteration. It's a kind of a death wish. Once again, survivalists will deny that this phenomenon occurs. Surely they are the last people in the world who crave the nuclear void. Yet although this denial may be appropriate to most survivalists, the phenomenon does, in fact, exist. It also seems to be increasing in frequency and intensity. As the survival movement grows more popular, the risk grows, too, for a kind of attitude which might well adopt as a motto the subtitle from Stanley Kubrick's *Dr. Strangelove*: "How I Learned Not to Worry and Love the Bomb."

A look at survivalist newsletters can give a sense of what's happening. It's not just the articles: after all, survival techniques and advice are the acknowledged subjects of such magazines. Rather, it is the unstated, implicit message in them. The cartoons and marginal drawings are suggestive: ghost-like men in radiation suits; families — kids included — armed like guerrillas; and of course the ever-present mushroom cloud...In some of the slicker magazines, especially, there seems a near-fascination with the spectale of nuclear explosions. One might almost expect to open a copy of *Survive* and find a fold-out in the middle — "Nuke of the Month." (The Fall, 1981, issue has something uncomfortably close.)

When I asked Robert Jay Lifton about some survivalists' fascination — even obsession — with nuclear imagery and their sense of impending doom, he said, "This is not so surprising. Death can become a powerful, almost erotic image." He suggested that this in itself wouldn't necessarily start in a deranged personality. "Are you familiar with the Japanese novelist Yukio Mishima? This was an extreme example of what could be stimulated in one's life. Despite his creativity, death became a source of erotic pleasure. Now it seems that people are identifying with the Bomb and its power in certain ways. There's a fascination with death-dealing power. It's sort of inevitable, in a way. Consider the *(Dr.) Strangelove* phenomenon — At the end of the movie, one of the characters rides a bomb out of the plane toward its target, and he gives out a big yell. It's a mixture of a desparate anti-nuclear cry and a kind of nuclear 'high'."

This isn't to say that survivalists actually want war. Most of those I've interviewed dread nuclear war as much as non-survivalists, and sometimes more so, since many have examined the likely consequences in more detail. But in gazing at the prospects before them, at least a minority seems to have succumbed to morbid fascination, and thus suffers from a paralysis of their critical abilities. Many of the militant survivalists show signs of real obsession with destructive devices. At best, it's a kind of war hysteria. At worst, it seems like thanatophilia — love of death.

But what of the others? What of the majority within the survival movement — the mainstream survivalists? What of the survivalists who store food and build a fallout shelter, but who have no intentions of hurting anyone? Since most fall into this category, these are the survivalists who swing the most weight and make the most difference. My own experience while interviewing people throughout the country is that few survivalists are paramilitary fanatics. Just as few are death-hungry nuts. They are most often workers, professionals, retired people, and families. Many are intelligent, concerned people who feel angry and helpless in the face of contemporary threats to their lives and happiness. All in all, their survivalist activities are a way of hedging some bets. Does this make their activities harmless?

Unfortunately, the answer is no. The reason is that survivalism, as a response to our problems, is understandable but inadequate. Far from helping people to face these problems, it allows them to back away from what is too often avoided already. I can only sympathize with the anger and helplessness which survivalists and almost everyone else feels. But the fact that survivalism is understandable doesn't necessarily justify it: survivalism provides an escape valve for some frustrations which could be put to better use.

An example of this is the issue of disarmament. Although many survivalists give lip service to arms control, most tend to see the task of negotiating pacts as too complex to be useful. Cresson Kearny explains it this way: "There are some people who think they'll get the genii back in the bottle, but I don't see how." Others have more specific concerns. As Robert Himber, editor of *Survive* magazine, recently wrote: "I hope to speak for all rational Americans when I say that we all want disarmament. It is how we go about obtaining it that should concern us. Let's not, as in the past, agree to dismantle our weapons while the Soviets agree to burn drawing-board plans for weapons." (In fact, the United States has never dismantled weapons as part of an arms-control agreement.) Still other survivalists express vehement opinions that disarmament, and not the proliferation of nuclear weapons, endangers them, and some speak of disarmament activists with great hostility; the most fashionable stance is for survivalists to dismiss proponents of arms control as "Doomies." Overall, it seems that survivalists regard substantive disarmament as a hopeless (if not actually undesirable) goal.

But this ignores the most basic reality of the situation. The United States and the Soviet Union possess some 17,520 nuclear warheads (*Time*, March 29,1982); Great Britian, France and the People's Republic of China also maintain their own nuclear arsenals; India, Israel, and South Africa appear to have built nuclear bombs (according to Niger Calder in *Nuclear Nightmares*); and the list of prospective candidates for the nuclear club includes Pakistan, Brazil, Argentina, Mexico, Columbia, Peru, Venezuela, Chile, Malasia, Indonesia, Australia, the Philippines, Zaire, Gabon, and Nigeria. Even West Germany and Japan — supposedly safe under the American "nuclear umbrella" — might choose to undertake their own nuclear programs. Whether any or all of these countries will do so is uncertain. The point for the moment is simply that little restrains them. The technology exists. Given the instability of world politics and the bad example which the two superpowers have set, the temptation continues to grow.

Survivalists consider the complexity of this dreary situation to be precisely what justifies their preparations. On the other hand, the outlook also argues eloquently against survivalism — and for antinuclear activism instead. Even now it appears debatable that attempts to "prepare" for nuclear war can succeed. How even the most comprehensive preparations could offer any worthwhile margin of safety in the future seems still more uncertain. At what point will people regard the nuclear arsenal as unacceptable? When eight countries possess bombs? Fifteen? Twenty-one? Fifty? When their explosive yield equals fifteen thousand megatons? Thirty thousand? Forty-five thousand? What does seem clear is that preventing the outbreak of nuclear war makes vastly more effective use of people's time and energy. The survivalists ask: what if the effort fails? This is a possibility. The basic truth remains that a nuclear war grows more and more likely if Americans and people throughout the world do not confront their own and each other's leaders and force them to stop risking everyone's lives in the name of "national security."

A sense of despair seems almost inescapable when facing these challenges. Our situation *is* desperate. It's understandable that even perceptive, strong-willed people would ask, "What else can you do but clear out?" I'd be a liar if I claimed to know what would guarantee survival in a dangerous era. Depletion of resources, hunger, overpopulation, and especially the arms race do, in fact, often appear to be almost insoluble problems. But what's the alternative to confronting them? Hiding in a shelter and waiting for the crack of doom? Whatever problems confront us, they certainly will worsen if people give up on them now and head for the hills.

Survivalists like to quote Aesop's fable of the Grasshopper and the Ant; it has become a touchstone within the movement. Perhaps the fable reassures them about their cleverness and foresight. But what if they have it backwards? What if stashing food and weapons turns out to be a waste of time? What if confronting the great problems of our age is the only real preparation for hard times? What if what seems like hope — preparation for the future — is really despair — giving up on the present? Who, then, will seem like the Grasshopper? Who will seem like the Ant?

The risk is that people may struggle to survive at any cost — even at the cost of their own membership in the wider community of men and women — and is so doing lose the humanity which makes survival worth our effort in the first place.

Bibliography

Abrams, Herbert L. and William E. Von Kaenel. "Medical Problems of Survivors of Nuclear War." **The New England Journal of Medicine**, November 12, 1981, 1226-1232.

Adams, Ruth and Susan Cullen, eds. **The Final Epidemic.** Chicago: Educational Foundation for Nuclear Science, 1981.

Aspin, Les. Review of "Soviet Civil Defense," by the Director of Central Intelligence (Report NI-78-10003, July, 1978), in **The Bulletin of the Atomic Scientists**, February, 1979.

Beeferman, Larry ed. "Cambridge and Nuclear Weapons." Cambridge, Mass.: Cambridge City Council, 1980.

Beilenson, Laurence W. "Selling Civil Defense." **Journal of Civil Defense**, December, 1981.

Blanchard, Wayne. "Industrial Civil Defense in Norway." **Journal of Civil Defense**, April, 1981.

Brownell, Will. "Gimme Shelter." **Survive**, July/August, 1982.

"Russia is Bullish on Civil Defense." **Survive.** March, 1982.

"Russia is Bullish on Civil Defense, Part II." **Survive,** May/June, 1982.

Calder, Nigel. **Nuclear Nightmares.** New York: Penguin Books, 1981.

Caldicott, Helen. **Nuclear Madness**. New York:
    Bantam Books, Inc., 1980.

"Civil Defense for the 1980's?" **PSR Newsletter,**
    Summer, 1981.

Clayton, Bruce D. "Get Ready, Get Set, Go Where? **Survive**
    Winter, 1981.

Life After Doomsday. New York: The Dial Press,
    1980.

"Nuclear Nonsense: "Dispelling 'Doomie' Myths."
    Survive, Fall, 1981.

"Nuclear Nonsense, Part II. **Survive**, Winter,
    1981.

"Planning for the Day After Doomsday." **The Bulletin
    of the Atomic Scientists**, September, 1977.

The Survivalist Directory. Mariposa, California:
    Clayton Survival Services, 1982.

"Survivalists, Guns, and Civil Defense." **Journal of
    Civil Defense**, August, 1981.

Crutzen, Paul J. and John W. Birks. "The Atmosphere After a
    Nuclear War: Twilight at Noon." **Ambio 11**,
    1982.

Culver, John C. "Dangerous Illusions." **The Bulletin
    of the Atomic Scientists**, September, 1979.

Day, Dorothy. **The Long Loneliness**. New York:
    Harper and Row, Publishers, 1952.

Director of Central Intelligence. "Soviet Civil Defense."
    Bureau of Public Affairs, Office of Public Communication,
        Special Report No. NI-78-10003, September, 1978.

Dumas, Lloyd J. "National Insecurity in the Nuclear Age."
    The Bulletin of the Atomic Scientists. May,
    1976.

"Enter: The 'Survivalist' " **Journal of Civil Defense,**
    April, 1981.

Feld, Bernard T. "The Consequences of Nuclear War."
    The Bulletin of the Atomic Scientists, June,
    1976. Fisher, Edward M. "Kamikaze U.S.A." **Journal of Civil
    Defense**, December, 1981.

Glasstone, Samuel and Philip J. Dolan, eds. **The Effects
    of Nuclear Weapons**. 3rd. ed. Washington: United
    States Department of Defense and the United States
    Department of Energy, 1977.

Goure, Leon ed. **Civil Defense: A Soviet View**.
    Washington, Department of Defense, 1978.

Gray, J. Glenn. **The Warriors**. New York: Harper
    and Row, Publishers, Inc., 1970.

Ground Zero Fund, Inc. **Nuclear War: What's in It for You?** New York: Pocket Books, 1982.

Handler, Philip et al, in the National Academy of Sciences. **Long-Term Worldwide Effects of Multiple. Nuclear-Weapons Detonations.** Washington: Printing and Publishing Office, National Academy of Sciences, 1975.

Hiatt, Howard H. "Preventing the Last Epidemic." **Journal of the American Medical Association,** November 21, 1980.

"Preventing the Last Epidemic, II." **Journal of the American Medical Association**, November 6, 1981.

High Risk Areas. Washington: Federal Emergency Management Agency (FEMA), 1979.

"Highlights of the Crisis Relocation Plan for New York City."**PSR** (Physcians for Social Responsibility, Inc.) **Newsletter**, Summer, 1982.

Himber, Robert. "Editor's Note." **Survive,** July/August, 1982.

In Time of Emergency. Washington: Federal Emergency Management Agency (FEMA), 1980.

Kaplan, Fred M. "The Soviet Civil Defense Myth, Part I." **The Bulletin of the Atomic Scientists,** March, 1978.

"The Soviet Civil Defense Myth, Part II." **The Bulletin of the Atomic Scientists**, April, 1978.

Katz, Arthur M. **Life After Nuclear War.** Cambridge, Mass.: Ballinger, 1982.

Kearny, Cresson H. **Nuclear War Survival Skills.** Coos Bay, Oregon: NWS Research Bureau, 1980.

Kelly, Brian. "Mormon Survival Spirit." **Survive,** May/June, 1982.

Kelly, James, et al. "Thinking the Unthinkable." **Time** March 29, 1982.

Lifton, Robert Jay. **Death in Life.** New York: Random House, 1967.

Kai Erikson. "Nuclear War's Effect on the Mind." **The New York Times,** March 15, 1982.

Long, Duncan. **Nuclear War Survival.** Wamego, Kansas: Long Survival Publications, 1980.

"Questions and Comments." Long Survival Newsletter, Vol. 3, No. 3.

Lown, Bernard. "Sounding Board: The Nuclear Arms Race and the Physician." **New England Journal of Medicine,** March 19, 1981.

McGrath, Peter, et al. "Thinking the Unthinkable." **Newsweek,** October 5, 1981.

McKeever, Jim. **Christians Will Go through the Tribulation...And How to Prepare for It.** Medford, Oregon: Omega Publications, 1978.

Medvedev, Zhores A. **Nuclear Disaster in the Urals.** New York: Vintage, 1979.

Murphey, Walter. "FY 1982: A CD liftoff? **Journal of Civil Defense,** April, 1982.

Nieman, T.F. **Better "Read" than Dead: The Complete Book of Nuclear Survival.** Englewood, Colorado: Quality Press, 1981.

Office of Technology Assessment. **The Effects of Nuclear War.** Washington: U.S. Government Printing Office, 1979.

Poos, Bob. "Terrene Ark 1: Utah's Earth Shelter." **Survive,** Fall, 1981.

Protection in the Nuclear Age. Washington: Defense Civil Preparedness Agency (DCPA), 1977.

Questions. Photocopied material from the Federal Emergency Management Agency (FEMA), Region VIII, 1982.

Saxon, Kurt. "The Art of Weaponry." **The Weaponeer,** Vol. 1, No. 1.

"Investment in Survival." **Atlan Formularies Survival Catalog,** July, 1981.

"What Is a Survivalist?" **The Survivor,** Vol. 5, No. 4.

Schell, Jonathan. **The Fate of the Earth.** New York: Alfred A. Knopf, 1982.

Sibley, C. Bruce. **Surviving Doomsday.** London: Shaw & Sons, 1977.

Singlaub, John K. "A Soldier Speaks Out on Civil Defense." **Survive.** May/June, 1982.

Sternglass, Ernest. **Secret Fallout.** New York: McGraw-Hill, 1981.

Tappan, Mel. "A Statement of Purpose." **PS** (Personal Survival) **Letter,** No. 1.

Survival Guns. Rogue River, Oregon: The Janus Press, 1980.

Tappan on Survival. Rogue River, Oregon: The Janus Press, 1981.

Tappan, Nancy. "Some Thoughts on Retreating." **PS Letter,** No. 19.

Thompson, E.P. and Dan Smith, eds. **Protest and Survive.** New York and London: Monthly Review Press, 1981.

Wigner, Eugene P. "Education — Key to CD success." **Journal of Civil Defense,** April, 1982.

Williams, Roger and Stephen Weston. "Civil Defense in Sweden." **Protect and Survive Monthly,** February, 1982.

"Civil Defense in Sweden, Part II." **Protect and Survive Monthly,** March, 1982.

Wolf, Marv. "Nancy Tappan: Survivor and Survivalist." **Survive,** Winter, 1981.

Yankauer, Alfred. "The Pseudo-Environment of National Defense." **American Journal of Public Health,** September, 1980.

Zuckerman, Ed. "Hiding from the Bomb — Again." **Harper's,** August, 1979.

"How Would the U.S. Survive a Nuclear War?" **Esquire,** March, 1982.

Zuckerman, Solly. **Nuclear Illusion and Reality.** New York: The Viking Press, 1982.